Can't Get **HERE** FROM

THERE

Can't Get **HERE** FROM
THERE

By

VINCE SANDERS

ISBN: 1-58721-928-X

This book is printed on acid free paper.

1stBooks - rev. 5/18/01

ABOUT THE BOOK

The National Black Network's first newscast was aired at 6AM July 3, 1973.

For fear our history will overlook a very crucial element of the civil rights movement, this book seeks to bring to fore some of the inner-workings of the nation's first African American owned and operated radio news network. The author was there from the initial broadcast through the better part of twenty years. Here he recounts the trials and tribulations of the struggle and subsequently the pride of triumphant success in the face of formidable odds. Many of these events and references will include a host of the nation's best-known dignitaries and celebrities.

Acknowledgments

Thanks to
Sinclair Clements

Special
Thanks to

ROY N. WOOD

LOVING
THANKS TO
JOYCE SANDERS

FOREWORD

The early 1970's might have been the most appropriate time in America's history to set up a radio news network for and about Blacks in the United States, more appropriate than any other time during the 2Oth Century. The riots of the 1960's, which had been installed as a legitimate dynamic of the Civil Rights Movement, were for the most part a thing of the past. The urban pockets of disfranchised citizens were no longer ablaze but the ashes were still smoldering. And everybody from the President to the Pope, and those in between, knew that this condition could not be trusted to remain status quo without progressive maintenance.

The legacy of Martin Luther King Jr., the century's most effective civil rights advocate, had ushered in cutting-edge changes to our social system. It was now the law of the land that Americans of African heritage could no longer be legally discriminated against at polling places, schoolhouses, lunch counters and all other venues where individual freedom may be exercised in the pursuit of happiness.

In the wake of Dr. Martin Luther King's assassination in April of 1968, then President Lyndon B. Johnson's National Advisory Commission on Civil Disorders reported, most forthrightly, that the United States was: "moving towards two societies, one black, one white; separate and unequal". So, the nation's leadership, especially the President, knew at least theoretically, the-test of-fire was still dangerously imminent.

These new laws would allow Blacks to seek a quality-of-life standard comparable to all other U.S. citizens and enjoy the rights of legal redress in cases of racial discrimination. In retrospect, one could conclude that the Civil Rights aspect of America's racial situation really began in the 70's; during those crucial and sometimes tense moments, when we were all trying to learn how to live under the new mandates. A wide variety of transformations were slowly evidencing all across the country.

For the first time in American History, A United States President would stand at the graveside of a very powerful Civil

Rights Leader and deliver the eulogy. It was early in the month of March 1971 when national Urban League Director Whitney Young, Jr. drowned while swimming in Lagos, Nigeria. President Richard M. Nixon eulogized Young while a throng of Mr. Nixon's cabinet members, along with many members of Congress, looked on.

Whitney M. Young, Jr., would eventually be replaced by a firebrand known as Vernon Jordan. He too, would rise to the heights of extraordinary renown as Director of the National Urban League and later as the controversial confidant to President Bill Clinton.

However, before the decade was over, President Nixon would later leave office under a dark cloud of shame. In the summer of 1974 Nixon resigned to avoid impeachment after having been battered by several forces for his role in the Watergate Scandal. Ironically, it was a black security guard at the Democratic National Committee Headquarters who was hailed by the media as a hero. Frank Wills, was the first to discover that there had been a break-in that was later traced to the Republican Party.

Meanwhile, the South was gearing up to send a peanut farmer to the White House. It was none other than Jimmy Carter who, in tandem with the first Black Man to be elected to Congress from Georgia since reconstruction, engineered a surprisingly triumphant run for the White House.

Andrew Young, was being elected to a third term in Congress as Jimmy Carter became President Elect in 1976. This White Country Farmer and a Black erudite former Civil Rights Activist, a direct disciple of the late Dr. Martin Luther King, Jr., were quietly laying the groundwork for a major political upset.

Members of the Congressional Black Caucus saw Gerald Ford as just another Republican who was soft on civil rights. Therefore, it would have been counter-productive to allow Ford to get to the Presidency. These considerations were abound when it became clear that Mr. Nixon would have to disgracefully step down, joining his beleaguered Vice President Spiro T. Agnew who also left office under a cloud of shame for taking kickbacks in his home state of Maryland.

When the congress was voting for an Agnew replacement, Andy Young started weaving his web. Having Gerald Ford in the Vice Presidential slot automatically cast Ford in the lead position for the Presidency. But Andy knew even then, that his one vote in the congress for Gerald Ford represented thousands of constituency votes for Jimmy Carter in the next presidential election.

For Andy knew that the nation was ready to elect a president with a strong civil rights agenda. It was a win-win situation. Blacks in large blocks, both North and South, would vote for Jimmy Carter while Whites all over the country were ready to commit to national leadership that could possibly heal the wounds of the 1960's.

What's more, the 70's decade presented America with a propitious "window of opportunity" in which to become of age and meet the stipulated expectations of its founders. And, the country's first Black news network would be as much a part of that dispensation as were the freedom marches, freedom bus-rides and the lunch counter sit-ins of the sixties.

Conversely, toward the end of the 1970's, there were signals pointing to a kind of progress everybody understood. Consumer marketing Guru, D. Parke Gibson released another one of his billion-dollar assessments of Black spending power in the US. His first book in 1968, reported that the Negro population spent $30 billion purchasing consumer goods. It was entitled: "The 30 Billion Dollar Negro" Gibson's second study was called: "70 Billion Dollars in the Black".

There was another study just before we rang in the New Year for 1970. Urban America and Urban Coalition, exactly one year from the release of the President's National Advisory Commission Report. It's conclusion: "We are a year closer to two societies. Black and white, increasingly separate and scarcely less equal!"

One of the world's funniest men successfully broke through the racial barriers of big time television in the 70's. Flip Wilson was the first African American to keep a show on the air with wide ranging sponsorship support. The racial atmosphere had forced abandonment of similar attempts by two other Black world class entertainers, Nat "king" Cole and Sammy Davis, Jr., before the advent of Wilson. Flip became a household name through the coinage of phrases such as: "The devil made me do it! "..."What you see is what you get!"

Two Young salesmen, one black and one white, thought they could induce Americans to laugh at their racial differences. The comedy team, known as Tim & Tom, told stories about white people without rhythm; but shied meticulously away from jokes about blacks who had very little more than rhythm. Neither Tim Reid nor Tom Dreesen, both of whom went on to become Hollywood stars, could attest to the efficacy of the concept. The team broke apart after a three to four year run.

This is only a minuscule list and in no way intended to rank or rate the issues and concerns of the seventies. But, the above items were certainly included and/or referenced as NBN reporters went about answering the network's call to duty.

Black News...mission towards human equality or another vehicle to enrich the established? This book will not address that issue except when attempting to explain the economic struggle of the National Black Network.

1

I have been waiting years now for either Alex Trebeck or Pat Sajak to ask the following questions, respectively: "The World Institute of Black Communications awarded it to corporations who advertised to Black audiences in an exclusive fashion." The Jeopardy contestant would reply thus: "What is a CEBA?" On Wheel of Fortune, Sajak would say something to this effect: " You will collect thirteen thousand dollars for solving the puzzle!....now comes the good part, there is another five thousand dollars for you if you can tell us who created the CEBA awards." Of course, he would not be as bright as the Jeopardy contestant and probably say: " An African Prince named Eugene Jackson." He would be only half right because Gene is not a full African Prince...he only dresses like one, occasionally.

"What the heck is a CEBA anyway?" I would very often present this query to my colleagues on the corporate side at Unity Broadcasting Network. I am not sure all of them recognized the selfishness fueling my critical remarks but it was all in family fun. Surely no one at the company could have been more of a CEBA beneficiary than I was.

The CEBA awards (pronounced SEE-bah) were created by our president, Eugene Jackson, to pay homage to major advertisers who were in fact spending some money advertising to black audiences but failing to budget proportionately to their sales among African Americans. But neither Sajak nor Trebeck would be held in contempt for not knowing this. Nor would they be chided for not realizing that Gene's primary motive was to convince non-advertisers that they too could realize improvement to their bottom-lines; provided they try to better understand the consumer patterns of the African American. Well, let's say that was just one of the primary motivations.

The central focus, however, was the ever-recurring demand on black media to justify their right to subsist in America through normal corporate practices.

Unity Broadcasting was the parent company to the National Black Network, America's first black owned and operated radio news network. When Gene came up with the idea of the CEBA (Communications Excellence to Black Audiences) awards, he was setting strategy against formidable odds. And to generate credibility for the awards, he was inspired to form the World Institute of Black Communications.

The mission of this new company was to free up some additional dollars from advertisers and their ad agencies through education. In other words, tell them over and over again the same results they found from their own research. This was essential to NBN's efforts to survive and hopefully thrive. But it would have been politically inappropriate for Gene to say that. So he said: " The World Institute of Black Communications (WIBC) is a non-profit corporation designed to increase the awareness of the ever expanding value of the Black Consumer Market to the total economy."

Therefore, it became a top priority for Gene to siphon off resources from his primary corporation to create a secondary service to function as a rescue system for the former. The author will take full responsibility for this flippant characterization. And, there is a good chance it will exacerbate opinions to the contrary.

Nonetheless, CEBA became Jackson's indelible hallmark and rightly so. During the fifteen years of its existence, the CEBA awards presentation attracted the participation of the country's top entertainment and sports stars of all dimensions, from Isaac Hayes and Gladys Knight to Nancy Wilson, Bill Cosby, Arthur Ashe and others too numerous to call by name.

In addition, there was always an adequate representation of politics and education. We also learned that Corporate America was indeed aware of the " gold in them there hills." This factor was evident in the profile of those who came when CEBA called. But drawing from past racial practices, these decision-makers were not accustomed to paying the requisite price for this particular burgeoning market. Jackson's CEBA would supposedly correct this.

All fifteen annual ceremonies were held at the New York Hilton Hotel in midtown Manhattan. That alone underscored the potential enormity of this thing called CEBA. As we became more proficient as promoters, down through the years, all of the leading advertising agencies and production houses and indeed major advertisers to black audiences, continued working for their respective opportunity to savor the distinction of being a CEBA recipient.

An observation of equal benefits was the industry fellowship spawned by CEBA. The black-tie cocktail receptions preceding the awards ceremonies coupled with the celebrity after-party in the penthouse at the Hilton, brought together the-most-unlikely-to-meet. Small black advertising agencies from anywhere, USA, rubbed shoulders with the biggest ad agencies Madison Avenue could muster. Celebrities galore! Actors, models, musicians, some achieved and some not so achieved.

So, what was so wrong about a marketplace stimulus that everybody thought was a great idea? Oh! Let me count the ways. For starters, it was an expensive situation. Top wrung recording artists for the entertainment and to serve as awards presenters. Even if the record companies brought the artists in for free, the amenities they demanded cost a fortune. Other major celebrities were flown in and feted just to prop up the image of the CEBA.

There were hundreds of categories of competition. This was necessary to assure against having one of the big advertisers and/or his advertising agency feel that his creative work for black audiences was left out. In other words bowing to the constant pressure of intra-industry politics. So, there were magazines, newspapers, billboards, album covers, posters, bus cards, radio, television and so on. All with separate areas of competition. About the only form of advertising not considered here would have been skywriting!

Now, who will serve as judges of this plethora of marketing creative? The experts of the industry, of course. Who are they and where are they? We found them! Many were in New York but hundreds were in other parts of the country. We brought them into specified rooms filled with ads for newspaper, magazines, billboards, radio and TV commercials, etc. Because of the manifold structure of a high level awards presentation, it is no simple task. At the very least it requires, among other things, a substantial budget and a commensurate amount of show-business savvy.

The initial CEBA awards presentation was without a doubt the most imposing and yet surprisingly effective. It would set the standard of things to come or not to come. Many hours of research and writing of scripts brought together a very impressive video module delineating the extraordinary spending options of the Black American female. A spirited narrative on her new-found income and the often overlooked influence she exerts in overall family spending decisions, left this inaugural CEBA audience asking for more. This was a strong message! And the big guys in the industry knew that Gene Jackson had made his mark in unveiling this better-educated more sophisticated mover & shaker known as Black Woman, "with a fist full of dollars."

But, the big guys also knew that this story had been told numerous times before. And even Gene himself knew how many times this message had been delivered to no avail, except maybe some utterly gratuitous platitudes for the messenger. Nonetheless, the consensus was that this modern-day messenger, Gene Jackson, had chosen a painfully ambitious means by which to remind decision-makers in the advertising world that we too are worthy. That is... worthy of being under consideration during the big meeting. The one at which advertising budgets are set according to media effectiveness instead ethnicity. In other words, include us in up front and spare us these extracurricular pressure tactics in the aftermath.

Less significant at the time but more foretelling was the unfortunate schedule of the first CEBA awards ceremony. We got started at seven-thirty one evening and ended at two-fifteen the following morning. Cost notwithstanding, the grand ballroom in the New York Hilton Hotel was, at that time, the only banquet facility in the city capable of accommodating twenty-five hundred patrons seated for dinner.

Even the sound system for such an event was a super configuration of dual consoles to drive speakers that were already affixed in ceilings three stories up from the floor. This in addition to the video and film equipment needed to showcase the competing advertising creative. Plus the various customized demands made by the performing artists to fit their individual egos. Pulling all of the elements together definitely exceeded our capacity.

Somehow, we got past the original CEBA awards presentation with driven inspirations to continue. The producer of the actual stage show whose minions spent months taking notes and hoping they would come to life at least a half hour before show time, was truly no bargain. In addition to their consistent inability to meet deadlines, the fee; even with a (knock'em-dead) discount, was more than many of us earned in an entire year.

So, how much do you think it cost to do this gig? Well, this is the question that sets up the main metaphor. By the time we got to year three, CEBA was no longer just a statuette to be handed to the winners for the best commercial or print ad to Black audiences; it was a tiger with a whip-saw tail that we could not let go!

The math is easy and rather revealing. When CEBA folded after fifteen years, we were selling out twenty-five hundred seats at two hundred and seventy-five dollars each. On one occasion down near the end, we had the Hilton staff bring additional tables and set them up in the lobby on the outside of the banquet hall. Needless to say, people who sat at these tables couldn't see who won which CEBA. That is, of course, if they were really interested. Many of them had taken the cocktail reception too literally.

And of course, there were hundreds of those seeing old friends for the first time in a long spell. This, on many occasions, raised the decibel levels of the ambient din to heights almost intolerable for anyone wanting to follow the progression of matters on the stage.

By this time, and indeed long before, the CEBA concept had captured the imagination of professionals at all levels of the advertising world. Unfortunately, that was one of the major soft spots in the life of CEBA. If you were not in the media professions, there was a strong chance you never heard of the CEBA. Particularly, if you lived outside of New York City, Detroit and Chicago. The other flaw was akin to the first. Because the support universe was limited to those in the business of creating commercials and print ads and a few endeavors related thereto, the thematic marketing pitch was beginning to sound like a story they had all heard too many times before.. Remember the one about the Black female and her influence over what is purchased in her neighborhood.

A logical response to that situation could have been, go ahead and change the theme. Not that easy. The Black Female angle was super safe for many reasons. Her role in the overall African American economic profile remains bolstered by a considerable number of other positive elements. Shift the spotlight from her and the risk deepens. For surely the accusatory tones of racism will ring louder when left naked for general analysis.

However, it was not CEBA's intent to cast the total problem of race at the feet of America's corporate advertisers. But, that question continues to loom when there is a failure to place advertising with black media companies, particularly those meeting specific performance criteria. The scrutiny intensifies when time after time major corporations attempt to rationalize the traditional practices of our society; especially, in the area of big-ticket commerce.

Conversely, it should be clear that CEBA's up-front motive was to do the same qualitative analysis on the entire Black American consumer spectrum. But, the effectiveness of the rollout-video module, the one that so adequately aroused the industry at our very first CEBA, could not be duplicated; not even by the people who conceived and produced the first one. Therefore, the marketing message did not change very much down through the years, even with an all-out expanded effort.

It was utterly important that we kept a certain level of entertainment associated with whatever message we did manage to emit. But the real difference in CEBA becoming the big deal it should have been was an unfortunately entangled affair. There was a failure to modify CEBA's mission after it became obvious that our marketing message had begun to lose its effectiveness. The re-defining of CEBA should have rendered it an annual celebration; one big party where all of the corporation biggies gather each year and drink toasts to the increased dollars spent in black owned and operated media. And collect their CEBA statuettes accordingly.

While the author continuously yields to the temptations of criticisms herein, he avers that CEBA was just right for the times. Conversely, it was difficult to ignore the manifestations of the self-fulfilling prophecy. While many good things were happening to Blacks in the media business, and we dare argue, some as a direct result of the CEBA stimuli, this great campaign for betterment was virtually running in place.

In about the tenth year, there was a conspicuous difference in the composition of the crowd. The ticket sales were constant. We sold out more often than not. But the persons in the seats did not quite meet the profile of CEBA's target objective. The decision makers at major companies had begun sending their secretaries who brought along their boyfriends and/or sisters. So, what do you do about this? This is analogous to a comedian losing his audience at the midway point of his act.

He is headed down the tube but cannot walk off the stage to save face because he is paid for a one-hour show.

CEBA was unable to continue its crusade for increased advertising in African American media for several self inflicted reasons. There should never have been a CEBA without a plan to take it to television. The first three years while we worked out the kinks and became immersed in the pieces and procedures, maybe! But year after year, having high powered actors, chart busting recording artists and celebrities from every category of entertainment and sports in the same room with the world's leading advertising executives and fail to make the deal; a grotesque misuse of resources.

The other problem found its roots tightly interwoven into our in-house politics. From the outset, CEBA had the miserable makings of a two-headed monster. While it was proper to

7

attempt to find some one among the staff to head this new venture, it was an unfortunate dereliction of corporate fundamentals to appoint two women to serve as co-directors of such a venture; neither having one iota of experience in the staging of a show.

Some of those close enough to the situation to proffer a valid viewpoint observed and opined that these were the early signs of the distrust that would plague Gene Jackson and Syd Small throughout the life of their business partnership. Gene's appointment of Joan Logue-Henry-Kinder to keep the CEBA basket was countermanded by Syd who appointed Adriane Gaines to keep count of his share of the eggs therein.

However, this represented only a modicum of the concerns about the total mix of CEBA. It did not appear to be any kind of secret or sinister personnel plan but CEBA immediately became a project bearing overall female influence, willy-nilly. Even the CEBA statuette, which is without question a genuine masterpiece, was created by the very gifted sculptress, Valerie Maynard.

And many of us could hardly wait again and again to hear the renowned actress, Ruby Dee, describe the cultural symbols inherent in the design and structure of the CEBA statuette. Ms. Dee's narration, kicking off the ceremonies each year, had the infectious appeal of a hit rap tune. Indeed, it was most refreshing to hear countless persons in the audience reciting the words in, a unison cadence, closely imitating Ms. Dee.

Even Terri Williams, before her incorrigible ambitions catapulted her to the showbiz level of the venerable comedian, Eddie Murphy, ran the CEBA awards for one year. This was during a period when the two co-directors, Joan Logue-Henry-Kinder and Adriane Gaines were backing off to play executive roles in the project. Terri was recently out of college and looking for a career opportunity commensurate with her intuitive skills. She came to the Network as an aide to company President, George Edwards.

As time evolved two other women became main cogs in the ongoing operations of CEBA. Lea Hodge, a friendly little Jewish girl who never confronted a problem she couldn't hug

8

and kiss away, was the outside producer; replacing her former employer, Carmine.   Lea, eventually developed the skills necessary to get the job done, rather expertly.

The banquet marketing was handled by a consummate pro when it came to putting fannies in the dinner seats. She knew everybody in the world who could afford to pay $275. for banquet ticket.   I was a company executive and served as announcer for CEBA all fifteen presentations...even I got a letter from her each year telling me where to sit if I got done with my chores in time. I kept thinking that our new president, George Edwards, would eventually take control of CEBA. He didn't and it remained a girl-thing with the two big boys watching through the eyes of their selected emissaries.

On the occasion when Bill Cosby was our lead talent for the show, I was mildly disappointed with the outcome. Somebody living on a space station near mars would be the only person in the universe possibly unaware of Bill Cosby's comedy, his uncanny ability to reel in an audience and work them into a belly-aching laughing seizure.

I considered myself a Bill Cosby fan of proprietary rank. Having seen him at the beginning of his career telling collegiate stories such as his chance to finally get off the bench and what does he do; goes to the wrong huddle and passes out weapons to the opposing football team. Further, dear reader, if you missed his take on Noah and the Ark from many years ago, I strongly suggest that you waste no time getting a copy of that video.

One Spring night in Indianapolis back in 1979, I thought for sure my favorite comedian was headed down the tube. It was literally the better part of 35 minutes before he got more than a courteous chuckle out of the audience. But, then the real Bill Cosby kicked in and appropriately left the entire house rolling in the aisles with laughter.

With respect to our CEBA presentations, it seems Mr. Cosby was unable to make any of the rehearsals except the one just hours before the show. He immediately began making drastic changes in the script; totally disregarding all the work done during the preceding rehearsal sessions. The unfortunate part of this scene was the absence of any structure that possibly could

9

have negated such an intrusion by even a potentate such as Bill Cosby.

And, of course, the CEBA brass was glad to have Bill Cosby at any cost. Therefore, they elected to allow Cosby's cuts and inclusions without protest. His changes didn't help the program, not in the least. And, on one of the occasions during the rehearsal when I offered only "slight" resistance, Mr. Cosby referred to me as "big voice" and gently emphasized that it would be his way or no way at all. And so it was.

Byron Allen! Now there is the name of a man who truly works hard for his money. Allen was on the show with Cosby. I think Allen was more than honored to be on the same bill with Bill but he would pay dearly for the privilege. For some unrehearsed reason, Allen and Cosby ended up on the stage at the same time. While Allen persisted in leaving lots of room for his role model to carry the impromptu performance, Cosby apparently wanted to make a comedic duel of the occasion.

However, let the records show that Byron's (mama didn't raise no fool). With the gentility of a knighted noble man, Allen ducked and dodged most of Cosby's jabs without even a hint of direct retaliation. But, that is Byron's long suit: subtle but dazzling footwork. I have yet to see him leave an audience in stitches but he continues working, and hard, I might add. Byron is such a seasoned performer now he seems never to work up a sweat. He is, without question, one of the nicest guys in show business.

In addition to Mr. Cosby, Adriane and Joan were able to pull together some rather stellar talent. Nancy Wilson and Marilyn Macoo headed our show bill twice each. The first of Marilyn's appearances was with her husband, Billy Davis, Jr. Gladys Knight and Isaac Hayes were lead performers for the first show.

Nancy Wilson left the CEBA staff a buzzing when she made it clear that she wanted no social privileges that would set her apart from the boys in the band. Nancy insisted that all refreshments, including those intended for the band, be sent to her suite; "because that's where they'll all be".

But, this was no surprise to any of us who had known Nancy through the years. Keeping her feet on the ground was her hallmark. Since the early years when I was a radio announcer and coming in contact with her, I decided that Nancy Wilson was one of the world's prettiest, sexiest and most intelligent women.

The stars were there for CEBA. The list is too long for total inclusion here but failure to mention some of the superstars would be disrespectful. Those such as Ossie Davis and his wife Ruby Dee, Tim Reid and his wife Daphne Maxwell Reid, Tramaine Hawkins, Patti LaBelle, Arthur Ashe and on and on...

On one occasion when super songster, Bill Whithers, decided to sit at my table in the downstairs restaurant at the New York Hilton, a decision he more than likely regretted. Bill and I had been going through the normal procedures of a CEBA rehearsal but no one-on-one conversation. In my earlier years as a disc jockey, I had unfairly selected not to give Bill the credit due as a performer. In spite of my evaluations, Mr. Whithers had some major hits, most of which were mega-buck crossovers.

Nonetheless as we sat, he made a valiant effort toward friendly conversation. His small talk included where did I make my home. I told him nearby Queens, New York. With a tone of delight, he said his daughter lived in Queens and that he was looking forward to seeing her when she attended the CEBA awards later in the evening. I don't recall the source of my discontent at the time, but his comment reminded me that I was terribly disappointed over something one of my off springs had done. As I started rattling off the sundry of problems parents are subject to...I could see the look on his face: "Hey Man, I didn't ask for all of that!"

Picking up on his body language, I quickly turned off the negative spiel. But he was a true gentleman and made another attempt at connecting. This time he would try to get through to me via my profession. After learning that I ran the broadcast operations for NBN when I wasn't the voice of CEBA, he began telling me stories about the days when he and Ed Bradley of CBS 60-Minutes fame were roommates. But the damage had been done. He must have concluded that: "This cat is in a really funky mood." Bill Whiters hurriedly finished his food and left. I am truly sorry Bill!

The year I asked Tim Reid and his wife Daphne to host the CEBA Awards, as fate would have it, I ran into Tim and Bob Johnson, the wizard who put together Black Entertainment Television, on the elevator. It was an amusing exchange. As I attempted to enter the elevator, Tim was emphatically pushing the button to close the door. My button prevailed and as I stepped inside we looked each other squarely in the eyes and burst into laughter. This of course, evoked a quizzical response from Mr. Johnson.

Without explanation to Bob, Tim and I continued blaming each other for the downfalls in our lives.

" I might have known it was you," He said.

I retorted "This has been going on for a long time, You're still in my way despite your achievements!"

The chatter became friendlier as he tried to demonstrate who I was without telling Bob Johnson:

"That's right Vince, You were there when all this got started."

"Yep...and I thought I had gotten rid of you but here you are again."

"Bob, this is Vince Sanders...he came close to ruining my career."

Bob, had noticed the logo of a major record label on my jacket: "Hi Vince, are you with that record company?"

"No...I'm with Sydney...The CEBA Awards"

"Oh yes, I know Sydney."

Then Tim began what appeared to be a bit of reflecting: "You know Vince, one thing I'll give you credit for: you kept telling me that I would not make it in show business until I fully committed my self to show business...you were right!"

"Yeah"...I left the conversation there. I didn't think it was the appropriate time for that type of discussion, with Bob Johnson being a stranger to me. Secondly, I knew why Tim was with Bob, trying to sell him one of those offbeat ideas Tim pulls out of the ether zone with astonishing rapidity. There was never an attempt to explain to Bob that I had been Tim Reid's personal manager when he started out as half of the Tim&Tom comedy team back in Chicago. I didn't see much of Tim beyond the elevator meeting over the next two days. During rehearsals, he was on stage and I was in the announcer's booth.

Through the forces of providential arrangement, it seemed we were able to save the best for last. Sinbad, The sensational comedic performer was the headliner for CEBA in its final year of 1995. It is perhaps safe to say this brilliant young performer was still in school when we staged the first CEBA awards in 1980. And while we are on the topic of brilliant performers, it is appropriate to mention that we came within a cat's whisker of getting Sammy Davis, Jr. to do CEBA. In fact he had personally promised me that he would.

As the story goes, the CEBA staff asked if I thought I could help in getting Sammy in the same fashion I had assisted in bringing the project to Tim Reid. Tim's former partner, Tom Dreesen, would always see that I got to hang out with him and Sammy whenever they were in New York or any other city in which we would find ourselves at the same time. Tom Dreesen was opening act for Sammy for many years before Frank Sinatra contracted Dreesen as his opening performer.

This particular day we went to see Sammy Davis, Jr. in his suite in a New York City Hotel. As we entered the room, the conversation following their usual hugging ritual, was thus: "Sammy, you remember my friend Vince, he is with the National Black Network."

"Of course, that's Unity Broadcasting, right? The CEBA Awards? OK. OK, same people right? Sammy goes on..."You won't believe this, I was just reading a proposal from the CEBA Awards."

I replied somewhat inanely: "You're kidding?"

"No, I am not kidding, I just minutes ago finished reading the proposal. How would I know the details of your project, if I were kidding?" He asked convincingly. Sammy then made his declaration: "I want to do that....I really want to do that! It sounds like fun!"

Meanwhile, Tom Dreesen is standing by and probably wondering if I had planned this to take advantage of his goodwill, which allowed me see Sammy in person. I had not mentioned to Tom on the way over that we had plans for trying

13

to get Sammy to do the CEBA awards. Frankly, to this day, I do not know how the written proposal got to Sammy.

Tom was as graceful as he could be under such circumstances. He didn't attempt to join the conversation. Instead he moved to Sammy's coffee table where one of the largest punch bowls in captivity sat full of fresh pistachio nuts. Tom grabbed a fist full of the nuts and continued prancing around the floor and chucking them into his mouth.

Soon the topic of conversation gravitated to other forms of small talk. I remained astonished at two levels. I simply could not believe that he willingly agreed to do the show without my asking...and: "My God! I had never seen that many pistachio nuts at one time in my life. What did it cost to get somebody to take the hulls off of them?"

I later learned that Sammy required this bit of specified ostentation in all of his hotel rooms; and why not? Mr. Davis will remain in our history books as the world's greatest entertainer.

When the CEBA awards were mentioned again, Tom and I were on our way out of the door. These were the direct instructions from Sammy. "Call Shirley Rhodes and tell her that I said I wanted to do this, she handles all of my scheduling." Ms. Rhodes was also the wife of Sammy's long time music director, George Rhodes.

Sammy's troupe was like one big family. There were 19 people who traveled with him on a regular basis and most of them had been with him for as many years. When we left Sammy's suite, I sincerely believed, and I think Tom was also convinced, that Mr. Davis really intended to do the CEBA awards. Tom was by this time a bona fide member of the Sammy Davis, Jr. entourage and knew all of these people very well. He, therefore, volunteered to mention to Shirley that he had witnessed my conversation with Sammy.

Several weeks went by after I had so proudly reported to the CEBA staff that it was a lock; Sammy Davis is all set to do the CEBA awards. The only thing left was the scheduling and that Mr. Davis himself would work that out with his assistant, Ms. Shirley Rhodes. As the tension of this telephone chase heightened, over a period of three weeks, I was able to get Ms. Rhodes to the phone only one time. I waited for her to get back to me and she didn't, despite my flood of phone calls to her as she moved around the country with the show.

During several conversations with Tom Dreesen I was able to glean that CEBA wasn't really a top priority with Shirley. I also picked up from the tone of his words that Tom was willing to go but only so far with this matter. And rightly so, it was of minuscule value to him. After all it was Shirley who played a large role in booking Tom as an opening act for Mr. Davis. That's a gig that few can have and nobody wants to blow it on behalf of a CEBA.

Finally, I was instructed to call Sammy's manager in Los Angeles. His response was the ultimate in superficiality. My one last call to Ms. Rhodes brought on the coup de grace. After realizing that I had not yet gone away, she resolutely said to me: "You got him to say yes, now dammit, get him to do it!"

I was stunned, to say the least. And, to this day, I haven't a clue as to whether Sammy worked me simply because we were socializing and he wanted let me down easy. Or, if Shirley was ticked off because she thought I went over her head. The other possibility is her thinking that I might have worked Sammy while his guards were down. Whatever the case, the records will show, Sammy Davis, Jr. did many great shows but he never did a CEBA show.

In all of its splendor...serving as a forum through which countless participants exchanged the essence of their dreams, yet unheralded but too inventive to ignore...CEBA remained, surprisingly, an enigma to some. It brought into convergence Black Professionals who had not yet been introduced, though they were in pursuit of the same ideals...how to market to the American of African descent by connecting with his culture without defacing his dignity.

There was an abundance of uncharted ground back then, during the transition from the turbulent sixties to the sanguine seventies. And, from time to time the question of trust would rise to the surface and generate high levels of discomfort among the ranks. Many Blacks in the industry found some discontent in the notion that the establishment was truly ready to cooperate under the new civil rights edicts.

Many of the Black advertising mavens forged their way through a maze of negativity at the major white advertising agencies, advising them on how to market to the African American. Then there were those who began seizing the moment with direct proposals to the advertiser, convincing him that there needed to be an exclusive approach to this fertile market segment. It's called an advertising agency owned and operated by blacks. Its sole purpose is to reach blacks on behalf of your products and services.

One such pioneer was Vince Cullers, founder of the Vince Cullers Advertising Agency. It was he who convinced his clients that they had to identify with the cause. The cause celebre was Black Power. Therefore, his clients had to be comfortable (or at least pretend they were) with the juxtaposing of the Black Power symbol (clenched fist facing forward and reaching upward) to their product symbols and images. And in some selected cases, an altering of proper syntax to meet traditional ethnic usage; a liberty heretofore unequivocally prohibited. It worked! Vince Cullers will be remembered among us, who were there back then, as the man who successfully sold black power to corporate America. But then, it was very painful to witness Vince Cullers vociferously complaining as he came down on the elevator leaving the ballroom. He sincerely could not understand why white advertising agencies could win so many awards at a black ceremony such as CEBA. He denounced the entire concept and said he would never return to the CEBA awards. This would have been a loss of major proportions had it held true. Certainly he was one of the trailblazers; setting a pace along with other giants such as Barbara Proctor, Tom Burrell, Byron Lewis, Frank Mingo, Caroline Jones, et al.

This was only the first CEBA awards ever. There were several spots in need of fixing. Some were adjusted and some were never diagnosed as problems and therefore never corrected. But, Vince Cullers did come back, and on at least one occasion, as co-chair of the CEBA awards.

So, if by chance, you should see a CEBA standing about in Manhattan or anywhere else in the world, please don't harm it; for it is truly one of our essential symbols of the Civil Rights Movement.

Overall, I think awards ceremonies are the greatest. On the occasions when I attended the TONY Awards, the saluting and celebrating of the best shows and performances on Broadway, there was no greater show business experience. They are always attended by a bevy of beautiful women, very rich men and vice versa. I was there on the night the "Odd Couple," Tony Randall and Jack Klugman hosted the ceremonies. And guess what? I was seated at the table with their personal manager, The grandest of all "Grand Old Men Of Hollywood", Abbey Greshler. Greshler was accompanied by his Confidant, Phil Gittelman, connoisseur of fine restaurants worldwide. He too was personal manager to several significant Hollywood stars.

This casual meeting with these two gentlemen would grow to such unpredictable proportions that I wondered how did it happen. I began to realize the strength of the relationship when Phil would call just to say hello and close with the "Big Guy" sends his regards. And on another occasion when I notified Phil that I was passing through on my way to Hawaii, a subsequent call from Abbey was in the form a reprimand for not allowing him arrange some Hollywood amenities for Joyce and me. Subsequently, whenever Phil and Abbey were in New York, for whatever reasons, it was dinner at a restaurant chosen by "Phil the food aficionado". I took the lead on one of Phil's visits and wrested control from his taste buds by taking him out to Tony Mazzarella's Waterfront Crab House. I think he was impressed…that's hard when it comes to Phil Gittelman and restaurants. But Phil is a fun guy with a heart as big he is…6' 3 ½" at least. On another visit when he said he had the entire weekend free for us to romp through New York City, I tricked him into foregoing a restaurant for street fair food on the westside. The night before we had spent some time at B. Smith's Restaurant where Essence Magazine was hosting a party in honor of Lionel Hampton. Sort of trade off, I hope.

A considerable amount of my enjoyment with these two guys was whenever I could cajole them into a mood to tell war stories about the movies and Hollywood in general. They were a wellspring and rightly so. Abbey was credited with bringing Jerry Lewis and Dean Martin to Hollywood for their first movie. It was amusing to say the least that even in the early days some of the pundits urged Abbey to separate Martin and Lewis long before the split actually did occur. Such outstanding performers as Don Johnson, Craig T. Nelson, Tony Dow, Sal Mineo and Kristoffer Tabori were among those whose business affairs were handled by Phil Gittelman.

In recent years before Abbey left us, Tommy (Tom Dreesen) had taken me by Matteos, the most renowned " watering hole" for Hollywood celebrities in all the world. As we walked in I saw Abbey.

I went to him expecting the kind of greeting we normally enjoyed: "Abbey! How are you?" He turned slowly: "OK, how are you?" and turned back to his previous focal point. Naturally I was disturbed by this, but I knew there must have been some reason for this behavior.

"Abbey, You don't remember me?"

"Don't make me guess, kid."

" This is Vince… Vince Sanders from New York." It didn't register. Realizing that I was on the brink of sounding rude I abandoned efforts to chat with him. All of 45 minutes later he burst over to our table: "Vince, how long are gonna be in town…does Phil know you are here? I'll call him and we can do dinner." Assuring him of my early evening flight, we agreed to do dinner on his next trip to New York. Phil later confirmed that Abbey was experiencing a memory problem.

CEBA

COMMUNICATIONS EXCELLENCE TO BLACK AUDIENCES

The World Institute of Black Communications is a non-profit corporation designed to "increase the awareness of the ever expanding value of the Black consumer market to the total economy." The institute has plans that include researching this market, compiling data on the consumption trends of Black Americans nationwide, and working with corporations and advertising agencies to increase the awareness of the profit potential found in Black communities throughout the country.

One of the greatest strengths of America, and there are many, is the competitive instinct best exemplified by our free enterprise system. It was out of an awareness of the positive value of America's desire to achieve and excel, that the CEBA Awards were established.

CEBA, an acronym for Communications Excellence to Black Audiences, is designed to award those corporations and advertising agencies that have had the wisdom, insight, and yes, the intestinal fortitude to pursue and persevere in an increasingly profitable and exciting market...the Black market.

Many of industry's leaders agree that this new award represents something meaningful. A broad spectrum of people were asked to participate, and participate they did. Chosen from the corporate advertising and communications communities, the CEBA Award judges toiled long and hard in an effort to pick the best entries in six communications vehicles: print, radio, television, sales promotion and merchandising, and outdoor and transit.

The CEBA Award was made possible by the involvement of agencies, advertisers, production houses, retailers and individuals who had the courage to participate by submitting entries and supporting the recognition of the segmented approach to the Black consumer market.

CEBA will take place alongside the other coveted awards in the industry which highlight superior achievement in communication.

To everyone who tried, who dared, we at the World Institute of Black Communications say THANK YOU!

CEBA is a registered trademark

19

Singer Nancy Wilson during one of her two appearances at the CEBA Awards in New York. She is joined here by Mrs. Joyce Sanders, wife of the author, Vince Sanders.

2

Before CEBA there was another animal (forgive the irreverent inference) called NBN, National Black Network. Oddly enough, a disproportionate number of organizations with missions related to the social ills of our country back then used the word National as a part of their descriptive nomenclature. Therefore, it became necessary on various occasions to explain that the National Black Network was not a non-profit group looking to provide free news and information for and about Black Americans.

NBN was, without a doubt, about commercialism. But, in the early seventies when it was yet an embryo with little or no life expectancy, I had limited knowledge of NBN and/or its mission until I began socializing with a Chicago chap named, Roy N. Wood, back in the late 1960's.

In those days, it was rare to find me in any kind of lounge or bar. But this particular evening was very special, as time would eventually prove. Roy had invited me. It was the beginning of the most exciting and rewarding two decades of my broadcast career. It was early fall 1972, and the weather was typically cool and brisk in keeping with the Windy City image. Roy Wood and I both wore top coats to ward of the chilly evening breeze. This was the day when he would explain the plans for a black news radio network called the National Black Network (NBN).

Roy was News Director at Radio Station WVON, the unequivocal bellwether station for African-American listeners in the Chicago area. He chose a meeting place that was easy. In addition to his radio job, Roy was also on the air for WCIU-TV. I was working as an anchor/reporter for NBC News. Both of these locations were in the Chicago Loop.

We didn't know each other well. It was our profession in common that brought us together whenever it did occur. He was News Director at one of Chicago's two black radio stations and I had just resigned as News Director at the other, (WBEE). Why we had not found reasons to socialize more frequently and share war stories, I don't know. However, there was always in the back of my mind the first experience. It was when circumstances initially brought me into close quarters with Roy. He was indeed a superstar commentator who endeared himself to Chicago area radio listeners through his unbridled commentaries. He always signed off his controversial editorials with an emotionally charged: "Now run and tell that!"

A group of newspaper and broadcast reporters had been invited to Montreal, Canada in 1967 to preview Canada's monumental preparations for "EXPO 67". 1967 was Canada's year to host what was known as the World's Fair. Roy and I were the only two African Americans in the group that visited from Chicago. Roy entered the plane somewhat later than I and moved onto the rear to select a seat from the few vacancies left on the chartered aircraft.

Therefore, there was no effort on either his part or mine to try and sit near each other. Frankly, I was somewhat intimidated by Mr. Woods bigger-than-life celebrity status in Chicago. So, if there were to be any friendship overtures, they would most likely have to come from him. And, eventually they did, albeit somewhat gratuitously.

Roy intimated that he might not have brought along the appropriate batteries for his imported tape recorder. In those days most radio reporters used German-made equipment. Therefore, it was not difficult for me to understand his situation. The following comments centered on how gracious the conversation, despite the various bus trips around the city of Montreal during the balance of the tour. He stayed out of my way and I made no effort to be near him.

However, it was to be at the end of this wonderful excursion that I would get a chance to see Mr. Wood in action. Within a period of 12 hours, Roy had utterly embarrassed me in the presence of our gracious Canadian hosts and sorely insulted my wife whom he had not met before we arrived back at O'Hare airport in Chicago.

We prepared to say goodbye to our hosts while dinning at one of Montreal's more famous restaurants. Its French language name was interpreted as "Grandma's House." The food was delicious. The official in charge of our visit, urged one of the lovely ladies in his group to bid us a good departure, in French without any interpretation, thereby preserving the romance of the language.

Those hostesses who had worn designated attire during working hours were now dressed for the evening. The spokeswoman donned a tightly fitting black and white plaid suit. This bit of ceremony for our departing was in no way less formal than all other occasions during the entire visit. Nonetheless, whatever Roy's motivation . . . he rose to his feet immediately following the young woman's good wishes to us and said:

"As a representative from the United States, all I have to say is . . .baby, the way you look in that plaid, it's enough to drive any cat mad!"

At first, there was an overwhelming hush over the room; these deafening seconds seemed like hours! And, when recovery finally did return to the crowd, our hosts were still gracious and began forthrightly appealing to Roy for a repeat of his remarks. From my seat, I was unable to determine if the subsequent din of the room actually prevented Roy from hearing that appeal . . . or was he quietly celebrating and saying "eureka" under his breath and didn't hear when they asked him to say it again. Another thought was that he might have realized how off base he was and didn't want to continue digging that hole.

Whatever the case, he never replied. This gave urgent cause to several of the other Americans (all white, save me) who felt they were street-smart enough to enlighten our French-speaking friends on "Roy's Rap."

Somehow, they lost track of the fact that everybody in that room spoke exceptional English; the Americans as a first language and the Canadian guides as a profession. Rational perspectives would eventually set in and suddenly all present would acknowledge that Roy had gotten past everyone in the room with his chosen usage of the English Language. For when the Americans came to their senses and were fully cognizant of the "lack of essence" in Roy's expressions, slowly . . . their faces began to redden and their tongues tangled . . . prompting an

23

almost abrupt end to efforts to interpret "Roy's Rap" for the Canadians.

Picture this if you will: A bunch of middle class white Americans in 1967, trying to explain to a group of white middle class Canadians what is being said by a black street-smart reporter, with a masters degree from The Columbia School of Journalism, who is hell-bent on rattling the establishment by ill-arranging conventional syntax while making sexual overtures to pretty white women.

I found it all rather amusing. Particularly the fact that Roy raised this entire ruckus from the rear portions of the dimly lighted room where, due to the hue of his skin, the full view of his physical image was barely discernable.

This was but one of those occasions that underscored the paradox in the persona of Roy N. Wood. Mr. Wood appeared to have found utter joy in the challenging of traditional middle class values. His profound wit, along with his diligent scholarship, allowed him the mental instruments to send reverberating shock waves through a room . . . with one short phrase. This, of course, is what I would learn of his personality much later in our friendship. Roy seemed poised to say the most unfitting things at the most improper time in the most unlikely crowd. And, oddly enough, with impunity. All of this appeared to have heightened his popularity in many a social setting.

The trip to Canada came to a close and we arrived back at O'Hare Airport where I would get another dose of Roy Wood's campaign against conventional behavior. After indicating that he would have to take a taxi home . . . I offered him a lift while jokingly asking if he would mind riding in a car with our station's call letters.

My wife and one of the announcers from WBEE had come to fetch me. The jock, Scott Gorman, as would most of the younger announcers in the Chicago area, was utterly thrilled to meet Roy Wood face-to-face. My introduction of the two became a handshaking, mutual admiration ceremony to turn one's stomach. To say they hit it off well would be an understatement. Gorman also had a penchant for shocking verbosity.

Once we were loaded into the station wagon, my wife Dolores, was formerly introduced. After we had driven a few blocks from the airport while Dolores brought me abreast of family occurrences during my absence, Roy began poking her on the shoulder and explaining that he was a professional baby-maker . . . and proceeded to give her a business card to that effect. He then asked her to pass it onto her girlfriends; " only those who did not exceed the age of twenty-one."

Scott Gorman found this extremely entertaining and was most generous with his comments of approval. As I peered at Dolores from the corner of my eye, she could clearly measure the degrees of my agitation. Immediately, she began making silent gestures in an attempt to assuage my ego, by indicating that she could handle it. After seething for a short while longer, I heeded her advice and ignored those comments and all the others of a similar nature that followed.

And, of course, there was another point of conciliation to be made here. Surely, she was less than comfortable with his inappropriate remarks but Roy was a celebrity in Dolores' eyes as well. It did not matter that she too was married to a radio personality. I subsequently reasoned: "Awe . . . what the heck?"

While dropping off Roy Wood at his residence, I was feeling very indifferent about the future of our relationship. I concluded to myself that it would be just as well that I never see this character again. But providence would not have it that way. Little did I know that this same character would be the conduit through which I would reach the most significant and sustaining plateau of my broadcasting career.

As the years rolled on, I worked with Roy at WCIU-TV in Chicago. Roy, Don Cornelius of "Soul Train" fame and lovely Janet Langhart made up a trio that hosted a news program for blacks called: "A Black's View of the News." Janet did the weather while Don covered sports and Roy was the news anchor. Shortly thereafter, Janet Langhart landed a spot with ABC, hosting a morning show in New York City. She had a good run.

While hosting two shows at WCIU, one interview/talk and the other a quiz show, on several occasions I filled in for Roy. The unfortunate circumstances of a heart attack dictated one of those substitutions. Just as he had always done, Roy rebounded and lived a very healthy and active life until he reached 81. He passed in the latter months of 1995.

And, of course, everybody knows of the history making triumph of, Don Cornelius, and his "Soul Train." This one is hard to write; you would have to have been there. But it is one of my most amusing memories of Roy and Don together. The two of them showed up at one of the major hotels in Chicago's loop to interview Sidney Portier. This was a black media thing. Black reporters were invited to an informal setting with the most achieved black actor in America. When I arrived, Roy had Sidney to himself, conducting an exclusive interview after having asked Don Cornelius to man the tape recorder. Finally, this is over and I will get my chance to talk to our star.

Suddenly, I hear incoherent mumbling between Roy and Don. Simultaneously, Sidney was fully demonstrating why he is who he is, strutting across the room and pausing to profile every fifth step. Now, I see him stop in the center of the floor . . . and lend a full ear to the conversation between Roy and Don. Roy is preparing to distance himself from what was developing into a very embarrassing scene. In his attempt to run for cover, Roy stepped away from Don and retorted with his foghorn of a voice: " you forgot to turn on the damned tape recorder!" Don never replied. He continued trying to find the recording someplace on the tape. Don knew that interview had to be somewhere on that tape and he continued searching.

Meanwhile, Mr. Portier stands on his tip toes and inquires in a loud voice . . . "What!?" He flailed his long arms outward, with upturned palms, and cupped his head and said as only Sidney Portier could . . . "My God man! I just gave you the interview of my career and you didn't have the tape recorder on?...incredible!' It was when Roy attempted to suggest taping it again that Sidney made it abundantly clear: "Absolutely not, I will not...that's it!"

By this time I am trembling and trying to fathom the premium placed on this interview. For a brief second or so, I had a notion to forego the interview and deny WBEE listeners the opportunity to hear "The Defiant One" talk about his movie of the same name.

It was about this time, Don Cornelius announced rather forcefully that he had located the interview on the tape and all was harmonious in the room again. My subsequent interview was conducted without a hitch. After Sidney's outburst, no way was I going to forget to turn on my tape recorder.

So, here it is five years or so later . . . Roy and I are in a bar talking about a national radio network owned by blacks and programmed for blacks. As it stands now, I don't feel indifferent about our relationship anymore. He is still the big guy at WVON. Janet is gone to ABC. I am working at NBC's Chicago station and Don Cornelius is on the way to becoming a mega-star with his Soul Train. But, Mr. Wood has called this meeting because, as I would learn later, of his respect for my work as a broadcaster. And, guess what? I am overwhelmingly flattered, by this guy for whom I had little regards in years gone by.

Roy is preparing to move to New York City to set up the National Black Network. This was the first I had heard of the project. It was at this time that he also suggested that I could join him. Apparently, he too had heard of my trails and tribulations at NBC. Roy was now holding vice presidency positions with two companies. He would be commuting to New York while maintaining full control of his news department at WVON. To say I was envious would be a huge understatement. I mused somewhat begrudgingly, "how wonderful it must be to be in such demand." Following a few words of gratitude to Roy, I assured him of my interest in joining him at NBN.

The winter had made its mark and was moving on. It is now the end of March 1973 but Chicago was still cold. The newly appointed News Director at WMAQ, Frank Barnako, invites me into his office and asked if I had taken any particular note of how badly he and I were getting along. For a moment I was stunned and speechless. Then came the strong urge to challenge his assertion: first denying that there was anything wrong with the relationship and secondly question his characterization of the relationship as one of a personal nature.

But, then I remembered something my Father left with me: "A man convinced against his will is most likely of his opinion still." Albeit, my views on the health of the relationship were conveniently different from his, it was he who had the "juice" and decided that my contract with NBC news would not be renewed.

It was agreed that my final day as an NBC employee would be June 16, 1973. In my state of distress, I concluded that it was better for all involved that we did not allow the debate to escalate. I suddenly remembered an occasion from the past when Barnako proved his true colors by telling me a polish joke as we sat across from each other in the newsroom. Then later in the afternoon, chiding me for laughing when another newsman told an ethnic joke involving Blacks. It was then that I realized that this was one of those fellows who makes up the rules as he goes. But, it has never been easy being the only Black in an otherwise all white situation.

For some unknown reason I did not rush to call Roy after learning of my imminent demise at NBC. Under most practical circumstances, this would have been the appropriate time to find out when he wanted me to report for work at the National Black Network. Inexplicably, I truly did not think of Roy as a source of employment until a close friend reminded me that I had been talking about moving to New York City to take a job with Roy Wood. This was after I had called every network in the Country. Now, I begin replaying, in my head, all of the Roy Wood conversations.

I remembered all of that black pride hanging on his every word as he explained the entrepreneurial significance of NBN. And, how there would be no expense spared with regards to new technology to get the job done. Thousands of dollars would be spent each month to purchase transmit-lines from AT&T. From all over the country, the best trained African-American news persons would be summoned to join this historical undertaking.

How ambitious! Particularly at a time when fewer than ten radio stations in the country were owned by Blacks. But, I was soon to realize that some rather impressive names at ABC had been involved in the research on this project. There was no question about the number of radio stations programmed to the Black listener. Whether there were enough stations owned by Blacks was of no consequence in this undertaking.

Very often in the sixties and seventies, projects of this kind were automatically accepted as a move toward leveling the playing field from a racial perspective. However, this one was a tough call. It had high potential to qualify as a "separate but equal" contrivance. Back then, it just wasn't that easy to determine if microcosmic components representing separate societies; one black and one white, were any better for the country than the other. In the final analysis, if the project succeeds, somebody is going to make a lot of money with a radio network offering specialized programming to a potential audience of 17 million people.

Meanwhile, reality is setting in and I am becoming conscious of the prospect of being unemployed very soon, if no connection is made. I attempt to call Roy Wood at WVON. The young woman in the news department doesn't know when he is scheduled to return. She does know that he is in New York moonlighting but she doesn't have a telephone number for him.

After tracking down a New York number and calling Roy, the beginning of the conversation was excruciatingly less than encouraging. In his attempt to be gentle, Roy uncharacteristically began stammering in a search for the proper words. In my mind . . . I rushed to judgement and reassured myself that this is the reason why I hadn't bothered to call him before now.

After regaining control of his speech patterns, Mr. Wood politely informed me that all of the anchor spots had been filled. A talent already located in New York had taken the one supposedly designated for me. I took a moment to collect myself, the pause was very obvious and graciously empathized by Roy. This was one of the rare moments when Roy was uncomfortable and choosing his words carefully. I could tell!

I was grossly unfair. After regaining composure, I forthrightly reminded him that it was he who had gone the extra length to tell me of the possibility of employment at NBN. Still lashing, I accused him of dropping out of sight and leaving me with no information regarding his plans. I had concluded that there was no job for me so let him have both barrels. Wrong!

Roy waited patiently for me to slow my attack before telling me that he was willing to go another mile on this matter. He promised he would call on the following day with a progress report. The call, nonetheless, came in closer to a week than the next day. It didn't matter. I was still waiting and feeling a little bit more positive about the courage and connection of my good friend Roy Wood. Mr. Wood is now back to his usual plateau of protruding pomposity, and I think it's wonderful.

With every phrase, during the phone call, he is convincing me of his clout in the organization. It's OK! We're making progress here. He evoked a huge rush of enthusiasm when he told me that he was scheduled in Chicago on the 16th. This was the very same day my commitment to NBC would end. He wanted me available for a meeting with him and Gene Jackson. "Who is Gene?" I asked. "He is the President!" Roy replied as if I should be punished for not knowing. I said: "Oh!"

The 16th of June 1973 was a Friday and my final day as an employee of NBC news. Ramsey Lewis was appearing at the London House with his Trio. A dear friend, Trudy Walton was program Director for WBEE and Ramsey had set aside a table for Trudy and her guests. She told me I could bring Gene and Roy along for the evening. When they arrived, as happenstance would have it, I was standing at the door with Ramsey. Roy and Ramsey were no strangers to each other. They greeted each other warmly and Roy introduced Gene. He was tall and very young looking to be a president. He appeared to be making a concerted effort not to be impressed by all of this. He was responsive but not friendly.

All in all . . . it was a wonderful evening. With Ramsey Lewis as the entertainment, no less was expected. One curious occurrence did leave me more than just a little bit concerned. Gene Jackson sat through the entire evening without one drink or a morsel of food. Many visitors to Chicago would kill for a steak at the London House. Particularly when Ramsey Lewis is picking up the check.

So, one might say that my employment interview for NBN began in the famous London House. Not much was said on the subject that evening. My two guests were stopping at the venerable Palmer House. I was a suburbanite, living some 25 miles from the center of Chicago's loop. They wanted me the next day for a continuation of my "interview." This wasn't easy.

As I awoke at some unreasonable hour the next morning in order to make a 7:30am meeting, I pondered two troubling issues: 1) Why in heaven's name did we have to meet so early on a Saturday morning? What on earth would they be doing for the balance of this non-business day? 2) What motivated Gene Jackson to sit through the entire evening, speaking only when spoken to, not drinking nor eating? I am now wondering if my prospective boss thinks I am a hot dog; inviting him to a world famous night club featuring an internationally renowned talent because I am some sort of a show-off.

I was on time and so were they. We are eating a big breakfast each, including Gene Jackson. We were slow getting into the primary topic. I found myself floundering in and out of very awkward bits of conversation about news coverage. For some reason both of them felt they should have to sell me on the concept of a black radio news network. They each took very officious stances in their promises to offer America quality newscasts for and about Black people.

Their side of the equation sagged a bit when each took turns probing me about my news experience. The interview lost its focus when they apparently tried to top each other by asking me a tougher question than the previous one. I made an attempt to keep things on track by politely reminding them that for the past three years, until as recently as yesterday, I was a full time reporter and anchorman for one of the nation's three major networks.

Breakfast was nearly finished and we had not made much progress with regards to arrangements for me to join NBN. I am still wondering why I had gotten out of my warm bed. No matter how I would raise the subject, there were no straightforward answers. Gene finally came up with the suggestion that I join them at a reception at the Johnson Products building. He wanted me to bring a tape recorder and demonstrate my reporting skills. I was deeply offended by the suggestion and found it rather taxing to resist telling him of my displeasure. I tried to get around the issue by not responding at all. At the end of the breakfast, he took another shot at it. He suggested that I cover the event for the National Black Network. I balked by questioning the wisdom of such an expenditure of effort when the network isn't yet on the air. This was also my opportunity to take another stab at getting the central question on the table. So I said, "with all due respect to Gene, I am reluctant to begin working for the network when I don't know my status with the company." He replied with a slight chuckle but did not offer any clarifications. We did, however, decide that I would attend the reception later in the afternoon but not as a working reporter.

Back in those days when black achievement in business was more visible through its scarcity than anything else, Chicago was home for two of the nation's most prominent black companies. Ironically, bearing similar names: Johnson Publishing and Johnson Products. Thereby causing some confusion among outsiders trying to distinguish one from the other. They both had erected opulent structures to house their headquarters. Johnson Publishing, of Jet and Ebony magazine fame, had established itself as the granddaddy of black commerce long before Johnson Products, providers of beauty aids and services, burst onto the scene with trend-setting fury.

The magazine company was located in the high rent district of Chicago's loop. The beauty-aids firm built its fortress some 80 to 90 blocks to the south where the residential population was then heavily Black. This was the site of the aforementioned Cocktail Reception. It was well attended.

Roy and I were proudly leading Gene around this mammoth crowd of Chicago's richest and most influential African Americans. We were in some cases advising them of Gene's entry to their ranks and in other cases warning them. Even with Gene and his first time ever black owned radio network as the topic; it was amazing to measure the popularity of Roy Wood among Chicago's elite. If anybody could get Mr. Eugene Jackson onto the correct social register Roy could.

It seemed only a short while before time had pushed us to the mid point of this splendid affair. Gene commented briefly on what he termed, "a high personal recognition factor," enjoyed by Roy and me in the Windy City. I thanked him. But Roy didn't hear him for he was busy schmoozing at a distance in the room.

It was nice of him to notice and mention. But my anxiety is about to take me down for the count. I am wondering, "when is this guy going to talk about my new job?" Then too, I am wondering if I've even got a job. My on-the-spot strategy was to remain close and conspicuously at his side, and at intervals, do something overt to remind him of my presence. The strategy had a painful flaw. He stepped on my foot once when I allowed it to wander in the path of one of his. He is a big man with feet of commensurate size.

As he continued shaking hands and meeting new friends, I hung in there. I needed an intelligent and effective way to remind Gene of our unfinished business.

Then the most incredible thing happened! Somebody walked up to us and said. "Vince, I hear you are leaving NBC. Where are you going?" "Whoops . . . what in the world do I say now?" Quickly, I reasoned in my mind "can't say I am going to the National Black Network. Moreover, I can't say I don't know." As I groped for the politically correct comment for this specific moment . . . I sought to buy some time by introducing him to Gene. Brilliant! Gene followed his "I am glad to meet you" with a resounding "He will be joining us at the National Black Network."

One could not imagine the degree of relief that single utterance brought. Residence of the South side of Chicago must have heard me exhale for miles around. During the flash of those seconds, I remembered the complaints fielded from fans who were loyal while I hosted a talk program on WBEE radio for seven years, then seized the opportunity to move to NBC news. They would call the NBC station in Chicago (WMAQ) and accuse me of abandoning the cause against racism. Whether or not my working for a black news operation represented that I made worthy contributions to the cause was not for me to say. However, for some reason, I wanted them all to know about my joining the National Black Network. In other words, "I'm back!"

As for my benefactor, the man who asked about my future plans, I sincerely wish I could remember who he was but I honestly can't recall. So, let this serve as my act of restitution: "Thanks Buddy. Whoever you are and wherever you may be. You enabled me to keep an unbroken supply of food on the table for Vince, Jr. And his seven sisters."

OK. So, I am hired. When do I report? Apparently, the President of NBN had not given any sincere thought to the topic. For when I broached the matter. He replied rapidly "Monday the 18th." Certain that he had mistakenly pictured the calendar in his memory, I said, "The 18th is tomorrow." He retorted "yeah! I need you there immediately." And turned away as if the subject was closed without possible redress. I thought, "My God! This guy thinks I'm a gypsy. "After several minutes of superficial haggling, we agreed that I would report for work one week later, on the 26th of June 1973. When they left town, Gene and Roy each said, they would work on some temporary lodging for me immediately upon their return to New York. The week had nearly slipped into oblivion when I woke from my state of anxious anticipation to realize that neither Gene nor Roy had contacted me to tell me where to have my mail sent. Gene had insisted that I must live in Manhattan. I never did question him on the real reason for this edict. I think it had something to do with Gene's perception of a needed image for network staff.

It didn't really matter to me. Finally, I get the chance to work in the Mecca of the broadcasting industry, New York City. However, some of the mirth derived from all of this began fading a bit when I was left no other choice than to speak to Syd Small, Gene's business partner. Through his secretary, Mr. Small informed me that he had not been apprized of my impending arrival, nor did he have any information regarding transport from the airport and my temporary lodging.

So, what on earth does one do now? My capacity to reason rationally may have been somewhat distorted at this point. However, of one thing I was absolutely convinced: this situation could not get any worse. " But then, what should you expect?" I asked myself. "You were interviewed for a job at the London House during the Ramsey Lewis Show and subsequently hired in the center of the floor at a festive cocktail party" Maybe the adage that admonishes thus: "water seeks its level" is applicable here. Or more simply: "you get what you pay for." Or whatever!…I am more than just a little concerned.

While talking to myself in those frank terms, I demanded that all future options be adequately weighed and thought through before, as my Grandfather used to say: "flying off the handle!" With this bit of tongue lashing, I was now regenerated and ready to go off and build a radio network. Albeit, a scary mess for me, I wanted to give the guys the benefit of the doubt and attribute all of this to a simple oversight. As for options, there were very few. One major consideration here was the discomfiting prospect of having to eventually tell my friends and family that the New York deal was off. What an ego buster! In quick order, my decision was to continue on to New York as if all was well. If things proved to the contrary, I would at the very least, be in a position to talk to the other networks, all of which were headquartered in the "Big Apple."

Canadian guide at "EXPO 67" in Montreal explaining the symbolic visions of the renowned "Geodesic Dome." This was also the event that brought Vince Sanders and Roy Wood together initially for an eventual tandem at NBN. Later in the evening, the guide became the subject of one of Roy's notorious roasts at dinner.

3

I arrived in the New York area on Friday evening. Impromptu arrangements had been made for me to stop at my cousin Frank Irving's place on Staten Island. Frank was very cordial. He met me at the Newark, NJ airport with his wife Beryl. After a quick tour of Staten Island, he then drove me to the Time-Life Building in Manhattan, the last known address of the National Black Network. This further prepared me for the following Monday morning when I would officially report for work. As it turned out, I would live in Staten Island for the next six months while continuing to look for suitable housing closer to my new job. After several weeks, I rented a house across the street from Frank and his family.

Monday morning finally dawned to end an extremely restless night. Sleep had been virtually impossible, what with the new surroundings and the anxiety of reporting to a new work assignment. After an abrupt rising to the occasion, I began my trek to the renowned Time-Life building. This would include a bus ride to the ferry landing, a ferry-ride to the battery Park section of Manhattan and subsequently the final leg of the trip to 51st Street and 6th Avenue. The dry run Frank had conducted on my behalf paid off. I arrived at the destination at 8:15AM.

Now, I stand before this large office directory, intensely searching for NBN's listing. Others in this huge lobby moved around and about me with utter abandon. This process had begun rather casually. My first consultation with the directory was a brief perusal, as I scanned down the alphabetized list of internationally known tenants. But, all of a sudden it struck me . . . there's is no NBN on this directory! I backed away from the directory, anxiously observing the people rush about me as though they had not a clue of my distressed circumstances. It was as if I expected someone to read the confused expression on my face and voluntarily offer the information I sorely needed. That didn't happen.

Then the solution came to me! I had inadvertently walked into the wrong lobby. I thought this was easily a simple mistake that could happen to anyone, in a never-ending sea of very tall buildings where each front entrance is virtually a carbon copy of the one next door on either side. Just like that, I suddenly discovered the key to my morass. All I had to do was go back to the sidewalk and enter the correct building; walk up to the directory and find NBN.

Well, Thank God! As I re-entered the same lobby following ascertainment that I was in fact in the Time-Life edifice, one of the doormen, who apparently had noticed some of my moves of befuddlement, asked if he could help? No sooner than the acronym, NBN, fell from my lips he said with infallible assurance. "They moved last week!" Frankly, I don't remember if I said anything at that point or not. But, there must have been something in my reaction that led the doorman to try and explain the inexplicable. And, of course, this kind of gratuitous compassion always comes out the same: "I'm sorry man, I wish I could help you." By now he is beginning to really measure my dejection. So, he summoned his colleague, who is within shouting distance on the other side of the lobby, and knows no more than he himself. Then, there is confirmation that he, in fact, has no additional information. As a matter of fact, this gentleman stared at me with a blank look on his face and reported that he had "never heard of the National Black Network."

"Wheeeee! ...This is getting worse." Not only did he not know they had moved, he didn't know they had ever been there. Then . . . another voice rang out from a short distance . . . "you talking about them black guys on the sixth floor, They moved up the street." For all of ten seconds, I thought we had broken the ice with some new information . . . but he continued "I don't know the address."

Just then, another member of the group retorted with a strong denunciation of uselessness regarding this last contribution. However, it was that last contributor who came up with the resolve. He immediately reasoned that, despite NBN's move, there is a great probability the telephone number is unchanged.

Therefore, the only thing left for me was to get over the fact that the firm I'm supposedly going to work for moved and never bothered notifying me. And, of course, learn where they had moved. Knowing that they had moved "up the street," as stated by the third voice in the lobby, was far from instructive. In an environment such as Midtown Manhattan, one needs to know the exact address and floor number. But his advice on the phone number possibly remaining the same, hit the jackpot! After calling and learning that the soon to be largest Black owned electronic communications company had chosen, 1350 Avenue of the Americas, as its headquarters, my new found friends, assured me that it was only a short walk away at 55th Street and 6th Avenue (A.K.A. Avenue Of The Americas).

As I took the elevator to the 19th floor, I had not a clue as to the splendor involved. It was later that I would be made aware that TV great, David Suskind, taped his show in that building. The American Federation of Radio and Television Artists (AFTRA) was headquartered there. The creme-de-la-creme among entertainment agencies, William Morris, was also perched at 1350. Others included, Arbitron, the nation's leading radio audience authority and Data Control, Arbitron's parent company. It was always rather delightful to share the elevators with the likes of Henny Youngman and Allen King. On one occasion, King jokingly chided me for calling the fire department to extinguish a blaze in his office across the street. He claims I interfered with the relationship between him and his insurance company.

Rhythm and Blues legend, Lloyd Price, also had offices directly across the street on 55th street. Given this list of neighbors, the National Black Network got started in a fairly decent neighborhood. On the first floor, there was a sizable screening room in which private screening parties would take place. Even Frank Sinatra, the chairman of the board, could be seen coming in and out on occasions. Actually, we were considered a part the virtual broadcast row . . . officially known as Rockefeller Center. The CBS headquarters was across the street on the corner directly facing the New York Hilton.

There wasn't notice in the corporate area of my finally arriving on the 19th floor, the 26th day of June in the year of nineteen hundred and seventy-three. I was truly impressed by the space. The broadcast studio was without a doubt a less than judicious use of space. But, it didn't matter much. There was more than adequate room for the various administrative offices.

Someone led me to the newsroom first and introduced me to my colleagues. There was John Lloyd, smooth resonant voice, young and handsome to boot. He had come from ABC. Another standout personality was Roy West. I mentioned these two chaps first because of their demonstrated ability at the typewriter and on the air as well. They made news writing and anchoring look easy. Roy West had also worked at ABC and I should add, while not as young as Lloyd, but certainly as good looking. Then, there was Hugh (A.K.A. Gene) Simpson, who had come from CBS. And, there was Tony Rousseau, as I would understand later, the more experienced newsman among them.

Tony had worked at both ABC and CBS. Tony was assistant director of news under Roy Wood. No one had informed me of this fact until Tony returned to the newsroom to find me seated at his desk. His forthright remarks included something to the effect of the company having not provided a chair and desk for me. After having established his rank, Tony assured me, however, that there would be the proper requisitioning on my behalf. Roy Wood had an office in a location which could be described as the center of activity. It was a cubicle, separating the tape operations from the larger portions of the newsroom. Joe Brown, also an alumnus of ABC, was in charge of tape operations.

Tensions are now beginning to ease, at least in my mind they are. I am on the job at last. In short order I am provided an employment application and directed toward a room where the employment process would be completed. In that room was John L. Herring, the company controller. One look at my papers, John is excited. We are homeboys from Orlando, Florida having attended the same high school. John had graduated in 1962. My class was ten years earlier.

Although, Herring was an outstanding football player for Jones High, I was nowhere around when he was throwing touchdown passes and preparing to enter Grambling University. There he would fulfill the dream of almost every young football player in the south, play quarterback under the legendary coach, Eddie Robinson. Before this moment, I knew nothing of John and he less of me.

With all the papers processed, I am now undergoing an anxiety rush. I am ready to get to work and let the powers-that-be see what I can do. Therefore, when I eventually did get in to see Roy Wood, my first words were about my on-air schedule. It was then that I learned that we were not going on the air just yet. And, until the schedule was set in a week or two, we would all do a mocked shift and practice writing and reading newscasts. I found this incredible but later reasoned to myself, what does it matter if you're on the payroll.

As we went through the early part of the week performing rehearsal newscasts, I was somewhat dismayed to find that there was nobody observing or critiquing the news writing nor the newscasts.

I confronted Tony Rousseau, the assistant News Director, he in so many words corroborated my earlier reasoning: What does it matter, as long as you're on the payroll? However, after learning of this chink in my armor, Tony abruptly found some problems with my newscasts. Much to my satisfaction, this did soon fade away and I had surely learned my lesson. It was very much like the old ruse we used to employ to help with "mic-fright"; don't worry about it! Nobody is listening anyway.

There was a very curious development as we moved toward the end of the rehearsal week. The assignment of shifts had begun with Joe Brown, the chief tape editor, taking more of an authoritative role than I thought was commensurate with his actual rank. So, we were all geared up to send down the network line a five-minute newscast every hour on the hour from 6AM until 11PM. Apparently, somebody forgot to do the math.

After all the New York boys had been given their assignments, which dictated that each anchor would have the luxury of two hours to write a five-minute newscast, Joe Brown and Roy Wood suddenly discovered that there weren't enough newscasts to go around. As I remember Joe, he was always a sort of champion for the underdog. So, it became abundantly clear that the Chicago lad would get the overnight shift while the home boys would be spread out over a slate that started with the 8AM cast and ended with the 11PM news.

Well, Joe brought this to Roy's attention just as I happened to have been passing Roy's office. I could hear Roy reaching for his "verbosity overdrive gear" as he instructed Joe to pencil me in at, 2am Monday through Friday. And, Joe complained in an explanatory manner, that there were only two newscasts left on the entire schedule, the 6AM and the 7AM. There were two issues here of major concern to Joe; the other anchors were required to perform four newscasts a day and Roy's colleague from Chicago would have only two each day. The remaining issue was more of a thorn for Roy than I had any occasion to realize, that being Tony Rousseau's perception that I had been imported by Roy to eventually unseat Tony.

Therefore, it would be in keeping with those purposes to assign his buddy to only two newscasts a day, albeit the dreaded graveyard shift. But, in spite of Joe Brown's efforts to keep the piece, the schedule remained as initially drawn. After getting in the newsroom at 2AM for about a week and realizing that this was a blunder that nobody actually cared about, I began shaving off a couple of hours and getting into the newsroom at about 4AM. And, none of the decision-makers seemed any the wiser while the fledgling network continued to amble along amidst its plethora of self inflicted distractions. Then, one day, suddenly, I am awakened from my naive slumber.

"Hey man! There is no structure here." My friend Roy is in over his head and these New York guys are making him pay dearly." As I began reflecting on the overtly flawed process of getting me from Chicago to New York, I concluded, there was ground for assuming that nobody was really in charge.

Or, whoever is in charge isn't very clear about how he is supposed to do this; That is, run a full-fledged line-connected radio network. One thing for sure, my buddy Roy Wood, had never worked for a network.

Further observation of these and other less than adequate situations had, by this time, begun to arouse ambitions that I had otherwise kept under wraps. My reasoning was somewhat along this line: "if Gene Jackson and Syd Small had chosen Roy as the head honcho, a high profile African American Newsman, but no network experience. I had worked for the NBC radio network. Therefore, playing my cards wisely could very well net me a spot at the top. Then, I thought: "all these other guys, who were conveniently located in New York, must be even more deficient in that regard." In all fairness to Roy, lack of network experience might not have been as much of a draw back as lack leadership acumen.

4

From the start, we had a rather decent on-air team. There was John Lloyd, Roy Darling (AKA Roy West), Gene Simpson, Tony Rousseau and yours truly. Roy Wood was also performing as an anchor. John Lloyd was doubling as a sports announcer. Joe Brown, the man in charge of tape operations, was a consummate pro at handling interviews and managing input from stringers at the small number of stations on our first list of affiliates. Joe had picked up his training at ABC also.

Nowhere in the country was there an abundance of African Americans with extensive radio and TV news experience. Roy Wood's role could have gone to either Mal Goode or Bob Teague or maybe Bruce Brown. But, chances are neither was available when the formation of the network was taking place. There could have been several more names with which I was unfamiliar.

Mal Goode's reputation goes far back to the days of his coverage of the Bay Of Pigs incident for ABC. Bob Teague first came to national prominence with his NBC coverage of the 1964 Republican convention from the Cow Palace in San Francisco.

Of these, Bruce Brown may have had the better skills. Though he came behind the other two during the late 1960's, Bruce's natural gifts of voice and aptitude, his constantly obnoxious display of scholarship notwithstanding, allowed him to move to an enviable position in the ABC radio news network organization. By the time we started NBN, Mal Goode was already retired from ABC. He joined us as consultant and senior correspondent at the United Nations. Bob Teague was still on the roster at NBC when NBN hit the streets. Some of us thought Teague might have been available. It was widely known that his book "Letter To A Black Boy" had caused some erosion in the momentum of his career path.

Whether Gene and/or Syd made an effort to get either Bruce Brown or Bob Teague to head the news operations at NBN, was not readily known. Roy's resume value was more attractive to the all important lending institutions than the need for him to actually know how to run a network. Some of this became very evident less than a month after the launch of the network. What with all the infighting, spearheaded by Tony Rousseau as he strove to have a definition of his role clarified, a blind man could see that my friend Roy Wood was in trouble.

When the shakeout came, however, its first victim was Tony Rousseau himself. It was an emotionless event. There were no outbursts of any kind nor do I recall any form of announcement regarding his departure. Whatever, Tony said or did to hasten his demise was not public information. Under normal circumstances one would have possibly concluded that Roy could breathe somewhat easier now with his nemesis gone. This was hardly the case.

Before Tony left, I had a few moments of good fellowship with this classic New Yorker; a second generation Haitian with a wealth of street savvy. Tony was a teacher of sorts. I was able to get a good look at him before he left the company. Invariably, Tony would make it a point let you know he had the information of which you were in need. And, the one element of his persona I found outstanding was his generosity.

It was Tony Rousseau who introduced me to one of the most expensive lunch one could experience in New York City and yet on another occasion, teach me how to attain the most inexpensive lunches possible in the Big Apple.

During one of his high moments of conviviality, Tony organized a foursome which included two of the young secretaries and me for lunch. When he began mentioning the Russian Tea Room as a nice place to have lunch, he was far beyond my current frames of reference. But, he caught me with my ego hanging out.

I couldn't dare allow these young ladies think that either I didn't want to or couldn't afford to have lunch with them. At any rate, when the check came in at about $150.00, Tony could see my lack of preparedness for this part of the occasion. He then reached for the bill and made an attempt to defray the full amount. But then, I talked him out it which wasn't difficult either.

46

On another day when Tony was in the organizing spirit, he asked me about having lunch at the then famed Americana Hotel located only a block away the MGM building. My prompt reply contained some comment to the effect of my inability to pay as we had at the Russian Tea Room. At the end of his normally overt and infectious burst of laughter, he assured me this would be drastically different. As I recall, two other persons including Roy West accepted the invitation. It turned into a hilariously unforgettable event as Tony led us into and through a maze of underground passageways. These were what appeared to be secret hallways, introducing us to the employee dining room in the basement at the Americana Hotel. Tony moved without inhibition, past a gentleman standing at the entrance and gestured for us to do the same, and it worked.

It was never clear to me whether the man at the door was security or management. It did not matter. The upshot here is that this cafeteria style eating arrangement allowed everyone who came through the line to eat, for only one dollar. And, you could return for a refill as often as your hunger or gluttony would dictate. Tony never let on how he knew about this bounty of fine food, virtually free, in the midst of Midtown's high-rent district. And Roy West said he didn't want to know. He accepted the situation as one typical of Tony Rousseau.

Through this entire episode, Roy West was in stitches with laughter. Roy found it easy to laugh even on his worse days. But, he found most of his humor through observations of the people around him. He would carry around in his head a caricature profile of everybody he came in contact with. Because he was so given to overwhelming bursts of laughter, Roy would register a very humorous study of one of our colleagues and couldn't deliver the punch line due to his being consumed by his own laughter. Roy West would almost daily provide me a good shot of amusement with his version of the feud going on between Tony Rousseau and Roy Wood.

Roy West and I grew closer as friends. It all started when one day he came to me quietly explaining that he too had to move from one market to another to remain in the broadcast business. He then explained that he had some disposable cash from which he would gladly advance a loan. Although, I had no need to take advantage of the gesture, he gained a considerable amount of my loyalty just through the offering. Roy West was impressive in other ways as well.

He owned a lovely home in New Jersey. His wife, Mary, an extremely pretty woman had a wonderful personality. They had a son and a daughter; it all seemed so perfect. I was very disappointed in later years to learn that this union had fallen on hard times.

Some of our other points of amusement could be found on the corporate side. Gene Jackson was listed as president while Syd Small carried the title of vice president. Of the 51% they owned, Gene had a slightly larger share, at least on paper. Then, of course, psychologically it was easy to view Gene as the Big Guy. His height is close to 6'5" while Syd is closer to 5'5". But, there were additional elements in the equation that did not necessarily qualify as common knowledge. They are as different in character as they are in physical appearance. And as we later learned, these differences would play out in the running of the company.

Under cursory analysis, Syd appeared to have had the edge but lacked the sophistication necessary to execute to his advantage. Example: a noteworthy number of the support and specialty staff members had come from ABC where Syd was once a Business Manager. But, there was no bonding between him and those persons who had been with him through thick and thin. His peculiar nature as a introverted individualist led him to keep a wall up at all times. And, most times you could tell that he was talking to you through a peephole in that wall. Therefore, the absence of fertile grounds for growth in trust and appreciation were woefully missing. It was as if he mistrusted everyone and gave no one any basis on which to trust him.

These traits played out in his relationship with Gene as well. The dramatic differences in the mental make up these men gave their company no chance of thriving. Gene's self-ordained mission was apparently to become the world's first black Howard Hughes. His ideas were twice the size of life and he hatched them by the dozens.

It was common knowledge among those close enough to know that Syd ascribed to a theory supported by the ancient adage: " A penny saved is a penny earned." Gene, conversely, thought that "two pennies earned suffices the same." So, Gene thought he was in business with a miserable miser and Syd saw his business partner as a tyrannical spendthrift.

How many times did we see Gene put on the table a package of strong suggestions for actions aimed at improvement or development within the company and Syd could not cope with his creativity? In many of these cases, Syd would excuse himself under a ruse of having to attend a very important meeting and never return to the our session. On some occasions, he would not make himself available to approve or reject the issue for periods of two to three days.

It would be way less than fair to let the foregoing criticisms stand without also pointing out that both Syd and Gene were very young men. Gene Jackson was still in his twenties and Syd had barely crossed the thirty year mark when they launched efforts to build the network. And they were embarking upon a trail that provided very few mentors, if any at all.

There were some moments in this bit of history when it appeared they were sincerely searching for a remedy. One of those occasions was when Gene went out and hired George Edwards as NBN's President. Not that we knew anything about Mr. Edward's ability. But, this seemed like the proper thing to do; let George serve as a wedge between the two bickering forces. You know, "let George do it."

George was hired in the fall of 1978. The Network was doing quite well. Recollection of when George was hired is easy for me for several reasons: 1) It was about that time of the year that I began dating Joyce Anderson, the single most important person in my life. I had been told about George but never got to meet him before he appeared at the annual black-tie Christmas Party held at Gene Jackson's house. Joyce and I were on our second date at that party. We were married in May of 1981 with vows performed by the Reverend Jesse Jackson at the PUSH headquarters in Chicago.

There was no way anybody, brought in from anywhere, could serve as president of the company any better than I. Obviously, Gene saw it differently. But it was a wake up call for me. Contrary to my thinking, a move over to corporate was never in the cards for me. In spite of all of my achievements in the development of the network, my bosses never saw me beyond the operational level of the network.

Among some of the things about NBN I will never forget is when George Edwards was hired. I was pissed! And, George did nothing to alleviate my concerns. He came in doing what he thought he was hired to do, that is run the entire company.

His first meeting with me came unannounced after he walked into my office and initiated what I thought was a social visit. In his normal eloquence, which many could easily mistake for arrogant verbosity, George solicited a profile of my duties. In hindsight, I acknowledged my reply as rude to George and could have led to harsh consequences. After all, he was president of the company.

At the time of this impromptu meeting, I didn't know if Mr. Edwards was "really" in charge of the company. But, I made an on-the-spot decision to roll the dice. "I'm Pissed remember!" So, I began using big words to counter his big words and alluded that he had been mistaken about the range of his assignment. Certainly, his jurisdiction did not include the newsroom. Therefore, it was not my job profile in need of clarification but rather his.

Suddenly, the room was filled with tension, similar to two fighters returning to their neutral corners after having thrown vicious right crosses at each other's heads. In the following few seconds, we were both reformed and realizing that we had been rather forward. Then we started powder-puffing each other. Nonetheless, he held his position and I didn't move to far from mine.

George came out a symbolic victor in this first encounter. In his departing remarks, the new president replaced his powder puff with boxing gloves again and said: " if in fact I don't have the power to fire you, I'll pretend I don't know that I don't and fire you anyway."

In a split second, I think to myself, "this boy is quick on his feet." As he stood in my doorway awaiting my reply to that salvo, I thought "Oh shit! What do I do now?"... "Hey! This is no time to cower, I must have been rather stellar in my performance as well. Otherwise, how did he get to the part where he is threatening to fire me? Can't quit now! All of this will have been for naught" I am not sure my voice wasn't obviously shaking when I said . . . "well, do what you gotta do."

But, one thing for sure, I had run completely out of machination medicine. I had no more wolf tickets to sell. George went about his way and I scurried to Gene Jackson's office to find out if the new president really could fire me. After our usual bit of banter, Gene learned of my meeting with George and meticulously assured me that I had little to worry about regarding George's power to fire me. But, his caveat was "I do expect him to function as president of the company."

So says Gene. Ultimately, George would become one of the many initiatives vaunted by Gene and eventually vetoed by Syd. This was a pattern that left an enigmatic veil over the image of the company for years. The network in its sheer essence was a 21st Century concept but stood a "snowball's chance in hell" of getting there.

George and I got on rather well down through the years. He eventually settled down to the reality of the situation. Neither of these owners was willing to leave him to running the company. Both were reluctant to leave George in the room alone with the other for fear of a shift in George's allegiance. At one point, he intimated that in spite of his efforts to the contrary, these guys had siphoned off every bit of inspiration he might have had. The president, therefore, was merely coming to work to simply get paid.

George was still there when Syd and Gene split up and went their separate ways. He remained with the network which was one of the assets assigned to Syd. There was far less of a chance that George would have any say so at all under this arrangement. They fought each other so fiercely that when Syd finally generated enough intestinal fortitude to ask George to leave, George beat him to the punch and said he wanted out.

It was just as well. For we were all at the point where we would face the eventual dismantling of the network as we had known it. The replacement for George was Jack Bryant who had been waiting around in the wings; doing everything required to remain in Syd's good favor. Of all the guys left from the early days, Jack appeared to answer Syd's needs more appropriately. They have faced several court battles together against their merged partners, Sheridan Broadcast Network. Together, NBN and SBN constitute American Urban Radio Network.

Twenty years later, this is the NBN vanguard as the end of the nation's first Black owned and operated radio news network had manifested itself. (From left) Sydney Small, Adrianne Gaines, Eugene Jackson, Joan Logue-Kinder and Vince Sanders. Missing from this photo are Roy N. Wood and Del Raycee.

5

Allow me to bring you back from the future and finish profiling the group of people I met upon arrival in New York. There was Sammy Ade, the chief Engineer. Not only had he worked at ABC but his wife, Maggie, was still on staff there. Sammy was all over the operations portions of the network quarters . . . he rarely sat at his desk; he would stand around in front of his office rubbing worry beads. His hallmark was repeating jokes Maggie had told him the night before.

Another ABC alumnus was Totty Elwell. She along with Sammy Ade, was one of three whites who joined the initial NBN staff. The other white guy is Del Raycee, who would introduce the company's first power struggle only after we had been operating for about a year.

I remember Totty as full faced, medium height, middle aged and stocky. She was a chain smoker and carried her cigarette with her right hand at a 90% angle. The burning cigarette was always about ear high. Totty was the traffic director. She was responsible for the scheduling of commercials in the newscasts. But, she was versed in quite few unrelated subjects. She too stood out in front of her office instead of sitting at her desk and would offer unsolicited comments on a variety of topics as they came along. Her office was right next to Yvonne Randolph who was the Personnel Director.

Randolph had been Syd's personal secretary at Time Life publishing where Syd served as Business Manager after leaving ABC. This tall thin woman who told everybody exactly what she thought of any given situation, at a moment's notice, was perceived as rather powerful because of her history with Syd. But she, as did several others, had to face the inevitable conclusion that the lack of a defined command structure, either by design or dereliction, would render havoc to her career path as well.

Ms. Randolph was one of those NBN victims who apparently found it hard to determine where her power began and ended. In addition to her stint with Syd at Time/Life, she was the support person while Gene, Syd and Del worked on putting the network together in a one room office donated to the cause by Time/Life. When she was dismissed in the sixth year of the network's existence, many observers were extremely surprised. As the company grew, she never realized the opportunity to grow with it as had been envisioned. Other personalities brought into the corporate area seemingly continued pushing her further away until finally she was released.

In the real power struggle, the one involving Del Raycee, there was some kind of dispute over whether Del had a partnership interest in the company. Most of us in the broadcast area had not a clue of what was going on. I became suspicious when after three weeks, Del did not return to work from what I had interpreted as a vacation.

As it turned out he was protesting the denial of his interest in the company by Gene and Syd. So, he called his lawyer and announced that he would not return to work until the matter was settled. He did eventually come back after about a year out of the office.

The way Del recounts the genesis of NBN . . . it was his idea. He and some other friend at ABC had done all the spade work before they understood that it would be better for all involved if some black guys were at the top. That's where Gene and Syd came in. Syd was no stranger to the people at ABC even though he had moved on and began working for Time/Life.

There were at least two versions of what went on in that squabble. Del said he was due 5 percent of the stock but Syd and Gene said he had none. To keep him in the family, so to speak, they would however, give him 3 percent. That's when Mr. Raycee decided to take a walk.

Syd's account of these developments was markedly different. He says Del contracted a severe case of "cold feet" while they were struggling trying to get the project off the ground. He asked out. And, they let him out, but allowed him to maintain an interim office in the NBN spaces which were being donated to the "minority cause." The closure point of this ongoing tale is that Del won . . . He was paid nearly a million dollars. He did return to work for awhile before eventually stepping out to buy a radio station Old Saybrook, Connecticut.

My relationship with Del Raycee had very wide extremities. There were times when I remained at a loss for assessing the state thereof. We didn't get along too well in the early years of the network. Looking back, there was a culture difference that sort of steered me out his way and he out of mine. I think he summed it up one day when he said: " anybody could sell you blue-sky." In other words, I didn't know how to play the game; office politics loaded with delusive tactics. He was correct. I always tried to play it straight. The degree of difficulty with such a notion intensified when I expected others to react similarly.

Therein lies the culture difference. Forget his being a New Englander of Greek ancestry and my being an African American from a farming family in Florida. It was a simple matter of miscommunications that divided us for the better part of a year.

I thought he had done me an egregious misdeed and reacted to it; he on the other hand found it strange that I would react. His theory was that these things happen all of the time and you simply wait for an opportune time to get even with your friendly foe. Eventually, when we were in the groove again, even better than before, I would jokingly refer to him as a triple agent in the company. He could convincingly change masks at a moment's notice.

Basically, Del is a very caring man who is sensitive to the core. But, there were those occasions when he would scale two ten-foot walls rather than have his true feelings revealed. Those are the times when it's risky to rely on him playing it straight. In addition, It is reasonable to deduce that he had to have some sort of defense for coping with his professional situation. His basic nature would not allow Del to be content with a second fiddle role as the third man behind Gene and Syd.

In the latter years, he would frequently complain about Gene and Syd accusing him of not understanding African American culture and thereby limiting his ability to get things done for the company. This bothered him deeply. The one thing Del Raycee did not want was anybody to think of him as unsophisticated; regarding all topics.

These are the moments when he evoked the most compassion from me but I never tried to assist him in putting those comments from Syd and Gene into proper perspective. During those days, I thought the guilt trip under which he appeared to be laboring was well deserved. He was getting a taste of his own double agent stratagems from his two black senior partners in the company. My guess is they used these tactics to offset Del's consistent nimble-footed moves.

This pressure caused him to constantly seek solace through trying to convince us that he was not given to racial practices. And that he did not have an identity problem working in a mostly black company. This situation was amusingly complex. I personally never thought of Del in a racial context until those moments when he felt the need to do or say something above the norm to prove his innocence.

Moreover, I would bet a weeks pay that neither Gene nor Syd really thought of Del in a racial context. It's an old trick; find a sensitive spot in a guys personality and the more he leans, the more you work him, that is until he topples or gets wise and correct his course. Del knew the script before these two guys got out of high school but somehow fell for their rhetoric; just as I did much of his down through the years. But ours was a strange love affair. Del and I sincerely appreciated each other.

One thousand times, at least, well maybe ten times, did he tell me the Dr. Wendell Cox story. The good Doctor was owner of our affiliated station in Detroit. He supposedly mistook Del for a light-skin African American. As the story goes, after years of playing golf with Dr. Cox, himself a fair-skinned African American who would have little trouble passing as a white, started a conversation that willy-nilly dictated Del reveal his ethnicity. By Del's Account, Dr Cox was literally stunned to learn that he was not a true "Soul Brother". On the occasions when he would recite this narrative, he would exude more pride than the time before.

In the bigger picture, however, Del and I were pals and moved harmoniously on several levels; mainly because we were the two guys with the most stripes as broadcasters. Therefore, he never had to say it to me more than once and vice versa. We both had worked at some of the smallest radio stations in the country and earned a working knowledge of almost every function at a broadcast facility. We could solve problems long before the others knew there had been a problem.

In addition, we both were cursed with larger than life egos and spent a commensurate number of hours intellectually protecting our opinions. He loves a challenge, an opportunity to beat the odds. A chance to gloat when it is clear that he out distanced the other guy. We were of similar spirits with a slight difference. I might have been willing to record a loss or two; he records only a win column.

Nonetheless, we took these attitudes beyond the walls of the network and into some fun places where we played as hard as we had worked. I was most amused watching Del pick horses at the racetrack while claiming to have some high degree of thoroughbred knowledge. Naturally, he would fancy himself as much of a poker player as I do myself. There was no question about his superiority on the golf course. It was only when he started getting older that I could even think of possibly playing to his level. He spent more time at the golf course than I did.

I am still holding the stock certificate representing 3000 shares in a company he talked me into buying. The small cap firm executed a reverse split of shares about two years out and nothing good has been heard about the company since. I couldn't tell if he was yanking my cord or not when months later I mentioned the stocks and he denied any knowledge of my having made the purchase.

In the bigger picture, there is more than just consolation in the fact that the very pretty woman Del is married to, has enough character to tilt the balance level. Ida Raycee and my lovely wife, Joyce, never had to fight through such social nuances as did their husbands. Down through the years we spent some wonderful times at the Raycees' palatial home on the Connecticut oceanfront and at their Florida home as well.

6

Keith Lockhart was another key player in the start of NBN. His job was public relations. For some reason he appeared not to be comfortable with his station. Somewhere near the end of the first year, he sent some kind of directive to the newsroom. As it would turn out, the directive failed to get the results Keith expected. And, he thereby, felt his authority had been skirted. So, he came back to the operations area to set straight the parties involved. I distinctly remember him passionately exclaiming that he was Gene Jackson's right-hand man. Therefore, when he speaks, it should be regarded as if Gene himself had spoken. Kieth's appeal didn't go over to well.

It was fortunate that I understood the source of his frustrations. All the while, I am thinking: "Gee! I thought I was Gene's right-hand man." By this time we were all meandering due to the lack of a defined flow chart of authority. Nonetheless, Keith Lockhart is one of the big success stories to come out of the NBN saga. Shortly thereafter, Keith started his own advertising agency. He is the principal partner in the major black advertising agency known as Lockhart and Pettus. His partner is Ted Pettus.

A couple of offices to the West of Kieth's office in the floor plan, is where the sales manager and his staff gathered to set strategies on the plan of attack. And, an attack is what it was in those days. Surely, there were no hordes of advertisers directing agencies to go immediately and place a hundred thousand dollars worth of commercials on that newly formed National Black Network. The sales manager was named John Williams. Our paths did not cross much in the short span of opportunity that did exist. It was in the first month or two in the life of the network that Mr. Williams was found dead in his apartment. So, he never got his plan of attack off the ground.

The way the story was told, After he hadn't shown for duty and there was no answer of the phone somebody, or several persons, from our office went to his apartment to find him dead.

John Williams was brother to a very important man among us in those days. Franklin Williams was U.S. Ambassador to Ghana and for a long time after his ambassadorship continued trying to bridge the gap between the U. S. and third world nations. A rare and a very special kind of guy, truly dedicated to the cause uplifting the entire human race. Coverage of his work alone, which in most cases was left out of general media, was enough to justify the need for NBN.

In the Public Relations department, Keith Lockhart had an assistant named Rina Artope. Rina was an attractive woman. This was difficult to ignore because my friend Roy West reminded me, with exclamatory expressions, each day. It was he who had also reminded me that she qualified as a "Redbone." Redbone was an early American cliché used to describe pretty women with Indian and African mixed race parents.

Rina also appeared confused about her assignment. Some of this, however, may have been by design rather than happenstance. There was speculation that Gene Jackson used the power of his office to lure Ms. Artope to his confidence and away from the influence of Kieth's leadership. This was not difficult to believe because as we all learned later, Gene had a separate agenda that widely transcended the everyday operations of a radio network. Gene needed a public relations person to spin his social viewpoints as well as keep the advertisers thinking good about the company.

It seems Rina, even long after Keith had left the company, was sent often to play the point while serving as an object of enticement to certain persons who had control of hefty advertising accounts. This fact came to light when Rina sought an explanation from me on why she was required to spend inordinate amounts time with C. Roy Jackson. C. Roy was a consultant on minority consumers for Kraft Foods. Her reason for sharing this with me was based on someone telling her that I knew C. Roy from my Chicago days.

This was true. But, the way I had known C. Roy Jackson was something I had tried to put behind me. Therefore, I couldn't be too encouraging with regards to his character. Nevertheless, she continued as instructed, with her assignment. It was important because Kraft Foods would become the sole sponsor of the Ossie Davis-Ruby Dee Story Hour, one of the true success stories of the National Black Network.

As this episode would turn out, in addition to keeping Rina busy with C. Roy Jackson, it also brought C. Roy back into my life after a decade. Mr. C. Roy Jackson, had fired me from my first full time on-air job at WMPP in East Chicago heights, Illinois. It began with a lawsuit that allowed the victor and new owner, Mr. Charlie Pinkard, to abruptly take control of the station. Pinkard brought in C. Roy as his new general manager and, of course, "the new broom swept clean!" On the day I was let go, Charlie Pinkard told me I could return, on the following day, to collect three hundred dollars in salary due me. I arrived about 11AM and was greeted by two large men at the door who were obviously armed and made no effort to conceal their hardware, at least not from me.

The two left me standing outside the building while they announced my presence to Mr. Pinkard who came out of his office and replied as though he had never heard of me before. Finally, I was allowed to enter the building while Mr. Pinkard explained to me that these kind of matters would be handled by his new General Manager, Mr. C. Roy Jackson.

At the same time he was leading me to C. Roy's office he proceeded to rap loudly on the door and push it open simultaneously. Much to his obvious surprise there was C. Roy with a tray of spareribs on his desk and a woman on his lap who was feeding C. Roy from the same bone she had bitten. The always-glib Charlie Pinkard has now begun to stutter. There is terror in the eyes of C. Roy. But the woman is still giggling as he pushes her up from his lap! Mr. Pinkard, after realizing that his words weren't coming out as desired, moved to deafening state of silence while trying to recover. As the moments moved on, he said to C. Roy:

"Mr. Sanders here says we owe him three hundred dollars in back wages, do you know anything about it?"

Mr. Jackson pulled open the lower drawer to his desk, peered into it, without touching a file or a single piece of paper, and looked up with a smirk on his face saying: " I don't see any record of it here."

Just as I began to feel the rush of blood to my head and incorrigible anger welling up in me, I suddenly remembered the two gentlemen who had let me in and decided to give credence to the adage: "discretion is the better part of valor."

Even winning a judgement against Seaway Broadcasting in small claims court failed to retrieve my three hundred dollars. Either fear or disgust prevented me from pursuing the collection process any further through the sheriff's office.

So, C. Roy Jackson surfaces in my experience once more. After learning of my position with the network which had won the contract to broadcast the Ossie Davis/Ruby Dee Story Hour, Mr. Jackson, notified Syd that he was concerned that there might be some problems with he and I working together on the project. According to Syd, C. Roy seemed relieved when Syd told him that was the first he had heard of the story. And that, he didn't think I would allow that kind of thing to interfere with a business arrangement.

7

Somewhere near the Spring of 1974 I began getting used to the fact that my career path had burrowed itself through to New York City. It was also about that time when I noticed the Chicago connection was unpredictably emerging as a very significant part of the network's development process.

As we entered the new year, Roy wood was asked to step down as Vice President of News. Roy Wood was replaced by Roy West but given the title of News Director instead of VP. If there was a formal announcement of this major change, I missed it! It was one of those situations in which something happened and it caught nobody by surprise because everybody knew something was bound to happen.

One afternoon as I was passing Roy Wood's office, I saw Roy West with a hammer banging nails for a book shelf. I took a tongue n' cheek swipe at this scene by referring to him as the new maintenance man. He abruptly informed me of his new assignment and apologetically acknowledged that no notification had been handed to the staff. He then stepped into his new office flashing all of his pearly white teeth while sliding into his new seat. We had a few jocular minutes together as I congratulated him on his rise to the top.

As I walked away, naturally, my heart was heavy for Roy Wood. At that particular moment, he was not around for comment. On the other hand, among all the others on staff, Roy West was the better choice for me personally. But, then I began to wonder what would happen to Roy Wood. He had completely severed ties with WVON in Chicago. Mr. Wood was now reaching his sixties.

My mind was eased shortly thereafter when I learned that Syd and Gene had not fired him. They subsequently asked me to find a spot in the anchor line up. This was not easy for Roy Wood especially after having profiled himself as one of the original shareholders of the company. But, over time he adjusted. Wood was always a valuable talent.

Now comes the moment I had been waiting for. I didn't know the strategy behind this move but apparently Gene and Syd had prepared Roy West for this eventuality. In causal conversation Roy West intimated that he had put my name in as the one to serve as his assistant. It was only a short time later when Syd would approach me while I stood at the news wire, reading through news copy preparing to write my next newscast. His comments were along the line of my claiming some expertise in the news business and that he would like to give me a shot at developing the NBN newsroom. His tone implied that I was being given an opportunity to eventually replace Roy West . . . but at the appropriate time.

After recovering from the shock, I tried to beat back the urge to yell "Eureka" as I told him I would like very much to help in any way I could. Meticulously, I got through this moment without too much show of emotion. Then I controlled myself long enough to point out that I could not accept the responsibility without all the other appropriate considerations.

He conceded and said he understood but ask me to trust him and allow time for "working out some things." The conversation was brief and directly to-the-point. We shook hands and he walked away partially explaining, in a voice that trailed away, "another formal change of command at this point would not bode well with the company's Board of Directors" . . .

Eventually, as the reality of what had just happened began to set in, I had to quickly reprimand myself: "Hold on stupid! There is absolutely no one in this newsroom or in the news director's office to whom you can break this news. You can't go into the office and tell Roy West that you're going to unseat him after all he's done for you. And certainly, you would be past stupid if you walked around the newsroom announcing your triumph to the staff members; a group among which you have few supporters, if any at all."

So, I had to work the balance of my shift with this look of the "cat who ate the canary" on my face. It wasn't easy. I must have drafted, in my mind, a dozen immediate changes that would take place the moment that it became appropriately clear that I was in charge. I did manage to complete the day without "letting the cat out of the bag."

At some point during the day, it dawned on me that I had been interviewed again, "NBN style!" This one took place at the wire service machine. The first had occurred in a bar with Roy Wood in Chicago, another at The London House Nightclub in Chicago during a Ramsey Lewis Show and a cocktail reception at Johnson Products headquarters, also in the Windy City.

Thinking back, it was rather ridiculous of us to squeeze two normal sized desks into a 10'x10' cubicle known as the News Director's office. The desks were placed facing each other. Mine had a name plate that read: Associate News Director? There was no room for any of the finer things of life like a big screen television. This arrangement, however, did serve to keep Roy West and me on the same page with regards to work related decisions.

Already, the new Roy and I are good friends. And the relationship is getting better. On too many matters administrative and otherwise, he overtly made disproportionate room for my points of view. In rapid fashion, the news staff was becoming sensitized to the fact that the Chicago Guy is taking over without censure. All of this came at a time in my life when a window of opportunity had to be seized. So, as Roy continued to give ground, I continued taking more.

The new chain of command revealed that Roy West and I shared similar passions for what we saw as dirley needed improvements in the way things were being done. We detected early on that there were several issues in the field that needed some immediate attention. Number one on the list was how do we get the affiliated stations to clear more of our newscasts?

We were newsmen. Our workplace understanding of a network painted a rosy picture of 100 radio stations or more; all of them broadcasting all of the NBN newscasts. Otherwise, a network did not exist. Wrong! Roy and I later found there could be several reasons why a station may maintain a position on the affiliation list. Principal among them was using the list to convince an advertiser that her commercials will be heard on all stations listed.

This was tough, particularly for major markets such as New York City, Chicago and Washington, D.C. Although, we all understood station relations to be Del Raycee's responsibility, Roy and I were fairly well convinced that there was a soft spot in those relations; the product being black and the salesman (Del Raycee) being white and so on . . . It was at this point that he and I felt it our duty to pitch in and help out Del.

What we didn't know, however, while the boys in the carpeted area commiserated with us to some degree, they were nowhere near as worked up about this matter as were we. For they were diligently working on formulas for clearance of the commercials without the newscasts. And were striking deals with the owners of these stations absolving them of any obligations to clear the news. Well now, Roy and I were sensitive enough to the "business side of business" but this places another spin on the social impact of this "black news radio network" thing.

Aha! So the dilemma yet prevails?" What do you want? A network with no affiliates because they are forced to air black news while their listeners are seeking the sound of black music? Or, do you want a black news network preparing news few people will hear because the affiliated radio stations will only clear the network commercials? Or, do you need black news at all? Sounds absurd? Of course, but it smacks of so much reality when the commercials are allowed to take precedence over the black news. And, to a large extent, that which is intended to inform and empower the disfranchised becomes a vehicle for further debasement. For many of the merchants who encroach upon the Black Communities of America are far from sensitive to the cause of mutually increasing sophistication through equal opportunities. And very often they invade the neighborhood, unfortunately through Black Media who themselves are weakened by large cavities in the playing field.

This is not a new problem. It is as old as the first African American newspaper ever produced in this country. Many of the pioneers of the Black Press were forced to maintain adamant positions against commercialized journalism. Without the support of advertising, mass media productions were a struggle

68

back then, and it is still a rough row to hoe even today. Major work has yet to be done to realize the full value of a specific genre of news and information for the urban areas. The key is fair advertiser support for good journalism. Simple.

Certainly, the situation has improved since the advent of the Civil Rights Movement. But as recently as June, 1999, The NNPA (National Newspapers Publishers Association) complained that a major maker of automobile tires has unilaterally refused to place ads in member newspapers for years; but found contentment as a sponsor of the NNPA annual convention.

However, It would be misleading in this account of NBN's reign to convey the impression that NBN's lack of opportunity to sell commercials was totally responsible for network's demise. Quite the contrary, NBN made money. Enough cash to subsequently purchase three radio stations; WDAS in Philadelphia, KATZ in St. Louis, and WWRL in New York City. But, despite NBN's claims to a 17 million African American listener base, like the African American Newspapers, corporate advertising was a piece-meal proposition.

There were several factors under consideration as Roy West and I sat down to map out operational plans to move the network forward. We worked very hard on the programming. I personally worked out extremely detailed parameters for the newscasts.

In general, electronic news coverage was already promoting the "five to ten second sound bite." We started delivering no less than eight stories with one to two sound bites and one voice report from the field in a five-minute newscast. Plus we had to pack in as much entertainment and celebrity information as possible. We had to fully acknowledged that stations on our network were more accurately described as: "music to the max."

The sound of our news had to fit in with the sound of the station without compromising the news content. We studied hard and long trying to make an appropriately informative newscast compatible with an hour full of driving disco sounds. In those days, whatever programmers agreed to add to their clocks had to be quick and delivered to capture the imagination of a wide range of demographics including younger listeners, the lifeblood of black radio.

In support of all other special efforts, Roy and I went to the nations capitol looking for the most expedient means of establishing a presence in the town where big news is made. We needed space for a bureau. Automatically, we concluded that the most beneficial arrangement would be one with our affiliated station in the Washington, D.C. area. When I tell you that we were in for the surprise of our careers, nothing could be so understated.

Our initial meeting was with the program director who wore doctor's smock. This bit of chosen attire in a radio station had something to do with his claim to being a superior format-fixer, or the best picker of records to increase the listening audience.

Be that as it may, our proposition was the wrong topic for him. This was never more obvious than when he refused to answer any questions on the value of increasing the number of newscasts aired from the network. The foregoing had met with such a dismal fate, we decided to shelve the suggestion of renting space to setup our DC bureau with the network providing national news updates while their staff concentrated on local coverage.

When the News Director finally joined the meeting, he began outlining the station's rationale. First of all, they did not need anyone to cover news for them. They were located in the nation's capitol and therefore had access to more national news than did we. Also, it made no difference to him that the owner of the station had agreed to a news affiliation arrangement with NBN. In addition, he had no space in which we could work as a bureau. Roy and I had to respectfully back away when he complained that the network was a threat to the job security of his news staff.

We eventually left the premises more than just a little disappointed, hoping we had not generated any negative reflections in the network's relationship with that station. It was then that we saw the need to visit the National Press Club in our search for bureau space. That was a better meeting. We were able to convince the club to rent us some space.

After returning to New York and informing our superiors that we had signed documents for the space and needed a check to consummate, the long procrastination period began. Unfortunately, there was never an NBN news bureau in Washington, DC, nor any of the other locations we discussed in our planning sessions.

Based on some other observations, less revealing than our failure to get the check, Roy and I finally concluded that we had been sent by Gene to set up the D.C. bureau without Syd's sanction. And he, as treasurer of the company, refused to release the funds. Syd was notorious for withholding operational funds. There was always a long list of disgruntled stringers around the country due to extremely late payments for the stories they had filed.

Despite Syd's tight-fisted protection of the cash, there did come that day when the fledgling network was threatened with the prospect of not being able to meet payroll. This came about during our second year of operations. Management was summoned to a meeting in preparation for passing the bad news on to the staff, if it became necessary.

As the years rolled out our future, all such close calls, including the aforementioned was avoided. In fact, some of the guys who had paid dues as I had, at small and less than solvent stations, often found it an expression of pride to mention that NBN did not contribute to such negative career experiences.

As we entered our fifth year, it was general knowledge that the differences between the two principal owners were beginning to take toll. It was predictable. They had two distinctly different modes of operating. Gene was clearly the innovator; perhaps veritable testimony to his degree in engineering. He kept Syd in an indignant scramble for position. His only defense against one of Gene's intellectual avalanches was to run for cover. Too often, crucial decisions were left looming after Syd refused to give in, ran away from a meeting, supposedly to answer an important phone call and never return for settlement of the matter.

Syd was a bit more difficult to decipher than Gene. His skills were mostly in accounting and that is where he spent most of his time, looking at the numbers.   Invariably, seeking to justify each and every issue by its literal monetary cost.

There is also a physical difference that falls far to the amusing side. Gene is well over six feet tall and has never played basketball or any other sports. Syd was a basketball player of star proportions while standing only about 5' 7"tall.

Eventually, the tug-o-war they played in the board room through the years was sometimes analogous to two notorious gamblers trying to read the cards in each others hands by looking in the mirror over the other guy's shoulder. However, it took all a decade (1973-1983) for science to cease challenging its own principles and allow the negative impact of incompatibility to finally render this duo asunder.

8

The NBN years yielded one remarkable personality who will always stand out in my memory, Dr. Frank Bannister. Frank first came to my attention one day when one of the New York guys on our staff gleefully pointed out: "that's Frank Bannister, Sports Director for our competition, The Mutual Black Network." Frank was Standing in the center of Yankee Stadium addressing thousands of people.

The adulation expressed for Frank by our guys left me dumbfounded. At first, I didn't get it. How could they be cheering this guy who is pulling off such a coup as presenting an award to baseball superstar Willie Mays with thousands of people, maybe millions, watching our competition on television.

They were more amused than anything else; utterly confounded by Frank's persona. Dr. Bannister's reputation putting him at the centerpiece of magnanimous events such as this was rather commonplace. But, when one tries to reconcile these achievements with the overall presentation of this jovial but not necessarily eloquent man, there seems to be a break in the required consistency.

As we all sat observing the ceremonies while various members of the staff who knew Frank Bannister filled me in on "who is this man?"...the occasion gave rise to another one of Roy West's patented humor-filled characterizations of "people we all know." After doubling over with laughter generated by his own thoughts . . . most of which he never uttered due to his own bursts of debilitating laughter . . . he concluded "you'd have to meet him . . . ha . . . ha ..ha .to understand."

Some weeks or even days later, there was some talk about trying to pirate Dr. Bannister from our competition. The discussion continued for several weeks amongst some heated moments of anxiety based on speculation that . . . "maybe this guy is commanding big bucks over there!" Nevertheless, the decision was finally made to approach the flamboyant Dr. Frank Bannister. That task would fall to Roy West and Me.

We met with Frank Bannister. It was easy. It was as if he knew we were coming. We had lunch and Roy did most of the talking. I am sure the topic of compensation did come up during that session but it was so fleeting as to be of no consequence.

And, of course, we tried to impress upon Dr. Bannister that central to our interest in him was his uncanny knack of being at the right place always at the right time. And, he in turn, assured us: "you ain't seen nothing yet."

If we thought what he had done for Mutual Black Network was spectacular just wait until he joined our team. In due time, Bannister moved from Mutual Black Network to the National Black Network. The not so explicit factor here is the most commonplace in the broadcast industry. If Frank did none of those outrageous things he promised, at least he would no longer be available to do them for the competition.

There were many things I would learn about Dr. Frank Bannister in the months ahead. Many of which were telegraphed on the day Roy and I met with him. I noticed that he wore big rings on his fingers. They were loaded with diamonds; the kind of rings entertainers and sports stars wear. His Cadillac appeared to have been custom made. It was pink and white. He appeared to have had a more than casual attraction to the color pink. He even had several sport jackets and matching trousers in the color pink. Frank's apparel bore little significance in the overall scheme of things except it hopefully underscored my light-hearted assessment of Frank Bannister as a very colorful personality.

One of the most impressive things about this guy was the aura of positive thoughts under which he lived. I never heard him discuss "positive thinking" but he would practice it everyday. Day after day, I would listen from my office as Bannister sat in the newsroom and talked about various major stars with whom he was on a first name basis. One would think that a first place reaction to this kind of name dropping and blowhard promoting of self would be an automatic turnoff to persons of normal intelligence. But, with Frank it was different. Some of his colleagues in the newsroom were unsure about which of the feats, espoused by this man, could he truthfully lay claim.

In 1974, the two of us flew to Kinshasa, Zaire to cover the Ali/Foreman fight. On that chartered flight, sponsored by Don King, were such sports figures as Heavyweight Champion Joe Frazier and former football great Jim Brown and a battery of other media persons. Frank moved well and it was difficult for me to actually tell if he was on a first name basis with all of them as he had claimed while back at the network.

Day after day he claimed some sort of fraternizing with Muhammad Ali. Almost every day, Bannister would sit at his desk and spew out stories about his call to Ali at home or Ali having called him at home. We do know that he had Don King at the network studios for an interview, so maybe it is possible for him to hang out with Ali. In fact, in those days, whenever I came in close contact with Don King, Bannister had promoted the meeting.

However, it was in Zaire that I was to learn that Ali did not know Frank Bannister. I was lodging in a villa down on the waterfront about two doors from Ali's villa. One sunny afternoon, Frank, who was living in the city at the only four star hotel in the country, wandered past my quarters. As I came out to hail him, he said he was on his way to visit Ali. Naturally I, who had never met Ali, jumped at the opportunity. As we entered the door, Frank, in the traditional style of a radio reporter thrust his tape recorder under the nose of Ali.

I was unclear about what Frank's question was to Ali . . . but I did see Ali turn curiously to Frank and ask him his name . . . and Frank replied in stern sincerity . . . "I'm Frank Bannister from the National Black Network." He was careful in an attempt to camouflage his lips as he realized I, whom he had told all along that he and Ali were longtime pals, was standing nearby and could hear this exchange. Nevertheless, the genesis of the Frank Bannister/Muhammad Ali saga happened at that moment. Just as Frank had apparently pictured it in his "going forward" dreams.

Bannister continued working on that relationship until it became a beneficial reality. In fact, in the late seventies, the

75

Muhammad Ali cartoon television show contained a Frank Bannister character who was Ali's sidekick in his episodes of crime fighting. I cannot attest to the success of the TV program but I do know it did exist and that Frank was Ali's crime fighting sidekick. Frank claimed the TV show was his original idea.

Remembering that day on the waterfront in Zaire, I am sadly reminded that it was during that meeting that Ali solicited my advice regarding his financial status. As all of those present in room moved around from one point to the other, I landed in a seat next to Ali. It was very clear that he was giving serious thought to pulling out of the fight game. He turned and said:

"Hey man, I got five million dollars in the bank right now, I could live off of that. What you think?"

I was a bit puzzled over his sudden introduction of the topic, and tried to read his mind before saying the wrong thing: So, I asked point blank:

"Are you planning to quit?"

"No, I'm just saying I could quit. I could live off the interest of five million, couldn't I?"

"Yeah...."

By this time somebody else who had overheard the comments while standing nearby entered the discussion. It continued along the same line with claims of five million dollars in the bank but never committing to the concept of leaving the ring for good. This was October 29, 1974, one day before he would triumphantly face off with George Foreman. This was a long way from the Olympic Games in Rome where in 1960 this warrior brought back the gold medal as a light heavyweight champion.

I had no difficulty understanding his contemplation of leaving the boxing game at that point; it was time. He had already had eighteen big battles since his return in October, 1970 after sitting out for three and a half years. He had his Heavyweight Championship status taken away in 1967 when he refused to serve in the US military for religious reasons. The unfortunate resolve here is he didn't quit then and continued fighting for several years in the future.

How far could he follow that notion to quit while on the verge of taking the heavyweight crown again? Not very far. So, the following night he took down George Foreman in the eighth round. Not only had he just reestablished his claim as the greatest prizefighter ever lived, there was an attachment of international politics accorded his decision to fight in Zaire.

In addition, some of America's most expensive entertainers had been to Kinshasa the week before. They were supposed to have been there during the week of the fight but there was a major snafu when Foreman postponed the initial fight date due to an eye injury. This was big time stuff with all the fanfare of a vintage Muhammad Ali. He couldn't quit at that point, five million in the bank notwithstanding. He is probably the most famous man in the world and he earned at least another five million for the Foreman fight. Muhammad Ali was just having fun talking about leaving the ring and watching the reactions of those listening.

So, when he and I moved near each other that afternoon in his villa and he asked again: "Whacha think man? Five million in the bank and what I'm gonna make for this fight, I could live off of that…couldn't I?"

This was tough for me. Mainly because I thought he should have had more than five million in the bank. But, I was also aware of the many rumors that he was the primary bankroll for the entire Black Muslim movement. Therefore, whatever money was left after Don King's lion's share went to Herbert Muhammad. I also knew how skilled this man was at getting people to love him through his childlike antics and expressions. So, I left his quarters thrilled to the gill that he would spend that much time with yours truly, and giving little thought that he might stop fighting after the Foreman fight.

Another source of wonderful amusement leading up to the fight was the continued banter between football great Jim Brown and Muhammad Ali: "Man that big dude's gonna kick your ass, look at his arms. All he needs is one good punch."

"Shit! You think I'm gonna let that farmer hit me. He can't move fast enough."

The climax to all of this repartee came at the end of the second round when Ali was reasonably sure his ring strategy was working. He had returned to his corner and sitting on his stool, his eyes scanned the ringside until they found Jim Brown who was there as a commentator for a cable TV company. Those of us in on this hilarious exchange between two of the world's greatest athletes were wiped out as Ali sat winking his eye at Jim Brown, gesturing to Jim that it was over and he should get ready to pay up.

Early on, we referred to Frank as Dr. Frank Bannister. But, what we have not yet mentioned is that he was also a former professional baseball player, that is according to his resume and his everyday conversations. Bannister held a Ph.D. from one of the prominent universities in upper New England. The grapevine take was that he had acquired it through an equivalency program. There was also a sustained cloud of suspicion over the history of his professional baseball playing days.

The story would bounce back and forth. He talked about his having been with the 69 Mets. On other occasions, he spoke of spending several years in the farm systems of the Pittsburgh Pirates. Frank's claim to have been a professional Baseball Player was a controversy he himself kept aglow with continued public references to same. And, it was this very issue that eventually separated him from the National Black Network.

When it was brought to my attention, by Syd Small with an ultimatum: "that something has to be done about it," I was presented with a copy of a newspaper article from one of the major papers in the south where Frank was most renowned. His work with Black College Sports had indeed earned him folk hero status. This sentiment was particularly strong in many areas of the South Region where most of the black schools were located. He had built this reputation While working at NBN. The young reporter appeared unduly motivated to expose Frank as a fraud. As in so many other cases, this young writer's research never allowed him to get to the good part. He never got a chance to know that, in addition to being the source of inspiration for the Muhammad Ali TV cartoon series, it was Frank Bannister who convinced Jet Magazine to publish weekly the ten best football teams at Black Colleges around the country. This may not have played as a big deal in some parts of our society but many of the coaches and faculty members at these schools would welcome any opportunity to energetically defend the charitable work of Dr. Frank Bannister.

During one of my visits back home in Orlando, a Black College coach who had attended the same high school as I, was walking around with a letter from Frank Bannister folded in his pocket. After we had gone through a not-so-convincing glad-to-see-you handshake, the coach who barely remembered if he had ever seen me before, came to life when I mentioned that I was a vice President at the National Black Network. But, this spark of appreciation for my achievements was just that; a short-lived spark that faded with my mentioning of the National Black Network. For in his mind, NBN was synonymous with the generous deeds of Frank Bannister.

There was no particular reason for Harold Smith to remember me. But, I would have had to have been a fraud to pretend I didn't remember his feats on the football field at our high school. When Smith pulled the letter from his pockets, he explained: " I am home on break but I am carrying this letter to make sure I answer it. This man has done more for young black college athletes than anybody I know." Not much time was spent on revealing the contents of the letter but this Frank Bannister fan went on to promise that he would be personally urging all coaches who got the letter to respond to Dr. Bannister's requests.

Finally, Smith got around to the usual stuff: "...So, you're making it in the Big Apple? How long do plan to be in town? Things are a lot different down here now. Make sure you say hello to Dr. Bannister for me." Somewhere along the line of this conversation, I got the impression that Frank was sending out another one of his self-promoting letters. I therefore resolved that upon my return to the office I could expect to see several of the responses as unsolicited pieces of correspondence from Black Coaches from around the country.

A considerable number of us at the network understood this element of Frank's Personality. He was very proud of what he did and some of his deeds were actually worthy of this kind of self ordained heroism. It was always amusing to me to see Frank in the restaurant on the bottom floor of our office building, announcing his profession loudly enough for everyone seated at the 50 or so tables to hear. He would stand up after having paid his eating bill and say: " well . . . I guess it's time for me to go upstairs and do my radio show!" And, if he were lucky, someone would asked "Are you on the radio?" Then, Doctor Bannister would "really" tell them about his radio show and all the celebrities he knew on a first name basis.

All this aside, Frank's virtues were more evident in his everyday social demeanor. During all the years I knew him, I never witnessed any sustained thoughts of anger or continued concern for people whom he felt had wronged him. Even his expressions of disappointment were quickly converted to that ever-flowing attempt to turn every situation into a bit of humor.

9

All the color at NBN was not limited to Frank Bannister's personality. At the very top, there was a personality that could very well fit the description of "unforgettable." Eugene Jackson, the founding president of the company, would be described by many as the proverbial "Bull in a China Shop." The adjustment for one's initial meeting of Gene is his height of six feet four inches along with large facial features. And, a big resonant voice to match his size. Depending on the nature of the gathering, he would either be doing all of the talking or most of it. He was never without an agenda and stood ever-ready to glibly promote his always controversial ambitions.

Several African-American media leaders often recount the story of Gene's decision to dismiss a very sought after advertiser, who until that meeting, found no reason to spend any dollars with the Black Media. This was a very familiar scenario. In those days, serious ad dollars didn't just fall out of the sky. Very often, the Black media owners would find it necessary to team up and go after a particular advertiser whose product could invariably be found on the shelves of cupboards in Black homes throughout the nation.

On this particular occasion, the advertiser had granted a meeting, only to have Gene become irritated with his manner of responding to pointed questions regarding the advertiser's failure to place advertising with African American Media; Gene announced that his time as president of a major radio network was worth some astronomical figure per minute and proceeded to walk out of the meeting. The meeting was either in such disrepair that it either yielded nothing from that point on or ended there. Some persons in that meeting thought they were on the verge of breaking the ice and this bit of vocalizing on the part of Mr. Jackson threw it off course.

However, as we would all eventually learn, Gene was given to believing his own press releases and overtly acting them out with total disregard for popular opinion. That, however, was only one part of the Gene Jackson persona. Because he apparently spent most of his time trying to come up with a better idea, than the last one he foisted on us, he came close to making our company an exciting broadcast facility.

I would venture to say that NBN probably would have been a different proposition with regard to its place in American History if Gene had been more of a hands-on president. He carried the creative touch but failed to focus. And, as is conceivable in all matters of creativity, not everything that qualifies as a worthwhile idea qualifies as a worthwhile business undertaking.

On one occasion when Gene thought I was challenging the viability of one his individual brainstorming sessions, he abruptly corrected me by urging me to understand that as president of the company, his job was to come up with the ideas. And it was my responsibility to get it done, no matter how ridiculous. In all fairness to Gene, he continuously cautioned us against notions to reinvent the wheel. Coming from Gene Jackson, however, this bit of proven philosophy was sometimes forsaken by the sage himself.

Nonetheless, it was Gene's visions that led us to know that in order to remain a network and continue gaining worthiness in the broadcast marketplace, we had to do the things that networks do. It is now 1976, a presidential candidate will be nominated from both major political parties and one of these will be elected President of the United States. The summer Olympics will take place on the grounds of our nearest neighbors to the North. Yes! Montreal was ready to "strut her stuff" yet again. It had been only eleven years before when the Canadians did themselves proud by staging the World's Fair, appropriately entitled "Expo '67." This was seven years before the birth of the National Black Network but it was like deja vu for yours truly when Gene insisted that we be there. I had covered "Expo 67" for a station for which I worked in Chicago.

By this time, the network is already nearly four years old but there was still so much room for growth. One major example, experienced news entities begin preparing for Olympic coverage about two years out. The Olympic committee wants each news organization to have submitted to them: 1) how many people you are sending for coverage ? 2) each must be specifically identified 3) specific lodging arrangements for each person 4) when will they arrive and for what events should they have credentials, etc. This information is required 10 to 12 months before the games begin.

President Eugene Jackson knew we were supposed to be there. Just as he knew we had to be in Kinshasa, Zaire nearly two years earlier when Muhammad Ali and George Foreman would be making worldwide history. Again, stuff that makes a radio network for and about Blacks more than necessary.

In retrospect, one could conclude that there was something prophetic in Gene's zeal to make certain that his young and inexperienced network be represented at these two events in particular: The Ali/Foreman fight and the 1976 games in Montreal, Canada. Those games graduated six African Americans who would go out and make significant marks as professional boxers: Howard Davis, John Tate, The Spinks Brothers, Leon and Michael, along with Sugar Ray Leonard.

There were other events at the Montreal games of special interest to the African American but there was no doubt that the record number of gold medals captured by the fighters was the Coup D' Gras. This, of course, does not denigrate the usually stellar performances of African Americans in the Track and Field events.

It was during this trip that I had my first course in learning: "who is this chap called Gene Jackson." One night when there was a hankering among us to find a disco, I remembered that I had seen one while wandering through the neighborhood. I recalled it being on the second floor and a staircase leading to it from the outside. We presented this description to passersby and they quickly told us how to find it and we did. It was a gigantic place with strict security; noticeable to me more so than others in our party because discos were not on my regular agenda.

There were five of us: Frank Bannister, his wife Virginia, Adrianne Gaines, who was working as Gene's assistant back in those days, Gene Jackson and yours truly. Gene had not had much opportunity to learn that I did not dance much nor did I drink anything more than an occasional glass of wine. Somewhere during the evening, it appeared he felt that I wasn't having as much fun as they were. He then began urging me to dance. I was rather self-conscious about a game leg which he evidently had not taken much note of. The more he solicited, the more I used circumvention to avoid revealing my real reason for not wanting to dance.

He appeared so concerned over the matter that I thought it best that I acquiesce to some degree. After all, he is my boss. So, I ordered a glass of white wine and had the bartender spike it with seven up. This caused more of an uproar than if I had continued not drinking at all. Nobody in this crowd had ever heard of such a sissified drink. While they danced I sipped my drink and enjoyed watching; mainly the Canadian girls. It was strange. Like a mild form of voyeurism. I was utterly surprised, these white people could do the wautusi with ease. They were so much better than their counterparts here in the United States who were still trying to adjust to the "Motown Sound" through American Bandstand. These Canadian girls were dancing as if they had been watching Don Cornelius' "Soul Train".

Before we decided to call it a night, I did get up and dance to one tune. Either to show good faith with Gene or it might have been inspiration drawn from the dancing Canadian women, who knows. And I did do some reflecting on the night at the London House in Chicago when Gene had done the same thing to me…sat through the entire evening without a morsel of food and nary a glass of wine. Now the question is whether I am guilty of just the reverse of my first faux pas…tried to get the company president to drink with me before he hired me. Now that I am hired…he wants me to drink and dance with him only to discover that I don't really dance and barely drink at all. Go figure!

10

1976 was a great year for the growth curve of the National Black Network. In addition the presidential nominating conventions, one in New York City and the other in Kansas City, Missouri, the United Nations was still adjusting to its ever growing slate of Third World Diplomats taking seats. Many of these representatives would for the first time vote on World affairs; and not necessarily following the usual line of conformity favorable to the Western Bloc.

The fact that the first of these monumental events would take place in the center of New York City was both a bitter and sweet experience. The Democratic National Convention was staged in the world renowned Madison Square Garden. This allowed our coverage without the cost of flying scores of people across the map. NBN was located exactly 20 blocks from the Garden.

The very first lessons to be learned involved the awesome influence of the three media giants in those days. As a new kid on the block we had to first understand that ABC, CBS, and NBC would get all the space they thought they needed. They had Carte Blanche to cover the convention inside the hall and all about the camp grounds. In similar fashion, the method of applying for coverage of the Olympics was the procedure for obtaining space on the convention floor.

This credentials procedure enables deployment of staff and reporters to cover as much of the backstage, on stage and around-stage as possible. Lucky for us, we would set out to report to the nation live from the Democratic Convention before the Olympic Games in Montreal. Albeit, a different form of difficulty, the conventions are as hard to plan as are the Games. But, everything is doubly difficult, I repeat, everything is hard in Madison Square Garden.

Nobody knew how or cared enough to tell newcomers how to get to any specific area of the building. Therefore, notes taken during the media walk-through had better include a map of the floor plan. Another condition that may have been more

85

coincidence than standard scheduling was the presence of a big Circus on both of the occasions we were involved in coverage at the Garden. After two weeks of elephants, horses and whatever else it takes to make up a big circus, having their way with a concrete floor, it behooves one to walk circumspectly and breathe only when necessary.

However, the really annoying problem at Madison Square Garden then and now is Labor Union control. One of our secretaries was stopped in the middle of the Garden floor and asked not too proceed without accompaniment of union personnel. I was later to understand that the box she was carrying was over the weight limit and must be carried by a union member. The box was about five pounds in actual weight.

After we learned that the three major networks would be assigned space inside the Garden upon which they would build broadcast facilities, we then realized that these arrangements did not include us. Large structures; some as tall as three stories up with all of the conveniences of their home base studios. It was at this point when we began to realize that we were on the cutting-edge of an evolution. The National Black Network was too small to be considered a true network on the scale of the big four: ABC, CBS, NBC and Mutual. Conversely, NBN was considerably larger than the independent radio groups which were limited to six stations by law back then. So a place had to be made for us, the new kid on the block.

We went back to the big huddle at our office and again entered Gene. Our fearless leader reminded us that we were in fact a network. And, that our mission was no less noble and essential than that of the big networks. For we too would be serving a sizable portion of the American population with news coverage of a convention that will choose a presidential candidate; who if elected, would be our listeners' President as well. And, because NBN is capable of reaching 12 Million persons, It therefore, should be assigned space proportionate to its market penetration.

But, after having been commissioned by Gene to go out and make it happen, yours truly was to learn the following: 1) Only ABC, CBS, NBC and independent broadcast operations such as

Westinghouse would be allocated space for building broadcast studios. Mainly, because they were the only ones capable of paying the freight for these privileges. 2) NBN was not listed as a network as such and therefore would receive those amenities allotted to the small independent broadcasters. 3) And, there was another level for these space allocations; owners of the sky suites permanently installed around the upper perimeter of the Garden would rent their boxes to media firms for coverage purposes. But this would happen only through approval from the House/Senate Press Gallery.

A rather hasty request from NBN for one of the sky-suites was posted and pushed aside just as quickly. They were all spoken for; this included eight units set aside for the Democratic National Committee. The real story here is that the National Black Network had begun a foray into an inner sanctum without prior notice. Never before had any all-black broadcast operation demanded consideration for privileges to be up front and out onto the main floor where all of the delegates are making decisions for their constituents.

As awkward as all of this may have appeared it was on a calendar commensurate with many other aspects of our society, nonetheless. Never before had there been such high anticipation on the prospect of Black voters deciding the outcome of a presidential election. Elected offices held by African Americans were at an all time high around the nation. So, many of these first-time-events were painstakingly forging their way through a labyrinth of falling obstacles.

There were those moments when yours truly felt it appropriate to give in and come back better educated and more prepared the next time around. After all, we could have conducted a piecemeal account of the conventions rather than the gavel-to-gavel coverage we had promised. There was, however, a major flaw in this kind of thinking. These conventions only come around every four years. More than that, there was too much happening in the social arena of the United States; and it was happening "now".

Our President was visibly astonished upon learning that the big wigs at the Democratic National Committee would hoard eight Sky Suites at Madison Square Garden. He dug deep for a barrage of supportive points to back up his forthcoming request. Gene Jackson convinced himself that the committee should release one of those booths to the National Black Network. Gene was very effective is this area. He could feed himself with his own rhetoric and become an incorrigible instrument thereof. There were those occasions, however, when his rhetoric just wouldn't fly. Nevertheless, his nature was always to walk away with an undaunted swagger; win or lose.

So, now our job is to appeal to the Democratic National Committee. We were no strangers to them on several levels. As the network continued developing, African American Democrats with clout in the persons of: Percy Sutton, Basil Patterson, Charles Rangel, David Dinkins et al were on a plateau of influence not to be ignored. These were all New York City boys walking shoulder-to-shoulder and overtly supportive of African American media developments.

Basil and Richard Hatcher, former Mayor of Gary, Indiana, whom I had known since his days in the Gary city council, were quickly gravitating toward the top at the Democratic Headquarters in Washington, D.C. My direct contact was in the person of Paul Brock who was a Deputy Press Relations man at the DNC. Paul had done his job well. Even before I had taken over the full mantle of operations at the Network, he had been very helpful in opening doors and making sure I had access to the Democratic luminaries from around the country.

Also in the National Office during those days and very helpful to NBN was Ms. Azie Morton who later was appointed Treasurer of the United States by President Jimmy Carter. Ms. Morton was the first African-American to be serve as US Treasurer.

Following a flood of phone calls and a few meetings, the Democratic Committee finally agreed to release one of the Sky Suites back to the senate gallery committee. The decision appeared to be unanimous but those persons involved in the process were annoyed and told me so. They were concerned that I saw the need to play the "race card" in getting across my point.

They contended that there was no inequality as I had implied and certainly none related to any racism.

Many of the decision-makers were African Americans bidding on behalf of the party and its leadership and not necessarily for or against the National Black Network. After all, these are not persons obscure to the political process and its myriad pitfalls of racism. Therefore, lifting the cloak from my sophomoric ruse was light work. And, I had to make clear the fact that I respectfully understood this. The fences were thereby duly mended.

Azie Morton was one of those persons expressly deserving of the apology I extended. Another friend was Ms. Hazel Dukes who more than once sprang to her feet to enumerate the virtues of the National Black Network and urge the committee to: "give this man what he wants because he is serving Blacks all over this Country." Ms. Dukes, in addition to her role at the Democratic National Committee, headed the New York state office of the NAACP and the New York Off Track betting system.

My next task was to assure the credibility of our on-air presentation. So, how do we do this? What we need is a scholar and/or renowned journalist who will work special assignment for this little new network. I was a little bit afraid of this one. A natural would be the illustrious Carl Rowan, syndicated columnist who had spent many years in the United States Diplomatic Corps. So, we made a list with Carl's name at the top.

If memory serves correctly, it was Paul Brock coming through again as he had done on many occasions before. Paul supplied Carl's telephone number and Carl responded after my leaving a message for him explaining what I needed. His first reply was that he would be at the convention under contract to his other clients but thought he would be able to include us in his scheduling. This aspect of our coverage became the easiest of all. Allow me to use an over-used cliche in my testimony regarding Carl Rowan, he is a gentleman and a scholar.

I don't quite recall the minutiae of our discussion on compensation but I do recall that it was harmonious. He asked what exactly did I need him to do, which was to sit several times during the gavel-to-gavel broadcast and offer sidebar commentary and record a wrap-up commentary for our stations to air the following morning. He told me his fee and I agreed and the contract followed. Carl was a dream to work with and this was the beginning of a mutually beneficial relationship. For Carl Rowan would work four subsequent conventions for us including the Republican gathering which took place in Kansas City, Missouri a month later. Carl also worked with us in 1980 at both conventions.

It didn't matter that he increased his fee each time around because he was worth it. And, what's more he became so involved in the overall content of the broadcast, he worked more than his contract called for throughout the entire presentation. It was primarily Carl and our own Mal Goode who attracted many of the heavy-hitters to our broadcast facility. Both of these men were known all over America. In addition to roaming the convention floor and keeping an eye on events close to the stage, Mal Goode provided a commentary for the stations as well.

In later years, another stellar personality joined our coverage team. Mr. Eddie Williams, President and founder of the Joint Center for Political Studies provided a very essential historical element to the broadcast.

The initial broadcast at Madison Square Garden in 1976 induced a good deal of pride among the politicians as well. They came to the Sky Suite in droves after the word got around. It stands to reason that Sky Suites in the Garden would be a bit more elegant than some others in similar arenas around the country. However, it became our modus operandi to request use of a sky suite in the cities where they were available.

And because we used the sky suites as hospitality areas as well as our broadcast booth, the sky suites became somewhat of a hallmark for us. The high level politicians could always duck into our party and have a cocktail while sitting for a brief interview. The NBN booth was also the place to stop for some good traditional African American food.

Television personalities Sue Simmons and Marc McEwen join in proving that the CEBA Awards is an Equal Opportunity organization. Here they present a CEBA statuette for its sister company to NBN's Vice President, Vince Sanders.

Renowned newspaper columnist and author, Carl Rowan hard at work during NBN's coverage of the political conventions. Holding the clock on Mr. Rowan is NBN's news department Chief, Vince Sanders.

11

The Democrats definitely did put on a bigger show than did the Republicans in the choosing of a candidate for President in 1976. The first leg up for the Democrats was their zeal to hold their party in Madison Square Garden, in New York City. This for me was an experience never to be forgotten. However, making the arrangements to cover the Republican Convention was far more intriguing.

Unlike the standing relationship the Network enjoyed with the higher-ups at the Democratic National Committee, The number of movers and shakers we knew at the Republican National Committee was next to zero. Which, of course, did not auger well for the hopes of pulling off the coverage with as much ease as we enjoyed with the other party.

But explore with me, if you will, the basis of this soft spot in our profile. In those days, there were nine African American members of Congress and only one was a Republican. Senator Edward Brooke of Massachusetts was rarely referred to as the Black Senator from Massachusetts. While on the other side of the aisles; major networks, whenever they found cause to quote one of the eight congressional members of African descent; a distinct effort was necessary to make this fact known. And, in some cases racial identity was more germane to the story than the quote.

So, you are a newsperson reporting on a story purported to be of essence to blacks, who you gonna call? A Black Congressman no doubt, who was more than likely voted into office by a black plurality. There was always the risk of adding too many angles to a story when you call a black Republican Senator who was sent to Washington by a predominant number of white voters. Unless of course, one of our reporters would be seeking a view from that side of the political picture. Frankly, I am not sure if Senator Brooke was sufficiently aware of the National Black Network. No discredit to the Senator, just conditions and circumstances of the times.

However, the foregoing should in no way leave the impression that all newsmakers covered by NBN were either Black or elected by predominantly black districts. As matter of fact our mission was founded in the reality of a need beyond the traditional coverage by general media. Therefore, we had to work all sides of the stream.

In preparation for coverage of the Democrats, we pleaded vigorously for recognition of my network as one on a mission equal to all others. In this scenario, all others were gearing up to cover the republicans in Kansas City, Mo. NBN would go also for more than a few reasons. Chief among them is that our sponsors paid for a package of two presidential nominating conventions. Also, it would be tantamount to shooting myself in the foot if I told the Senate Press Gallery committee that I needed fewer accommodations to cover the Republicans than for the Democrats.

For the record, let it be understood that there were never any such notions. In fact, there were simultaneous preparations for both events in some respects. But the scarcity of African Americans involved in the Republican process was blatantly obvious.

Among the stellar list of Democratic Dignitaries would be the Reverend Jesse Jackson, eight black congresspersons, ten black mayors and possibly a thousand or more of who held positions, either elective or appointive, in their respective states, counties and cities. And thousands more African American dignitaries plus there was no question about the strength of Jimmy Carter's civil rights platform. An easy call, for sure. Superstar status blacks in the Republican Party were few and far in between.

None of this was trivial as some may suggest. American media and politics needed a fix along racial lines. Very often, some major news guy from the other nets, after getting to know me well enough to feel comfortable in addressing the topic, would ask: "Vince, what do you consider black news . . . I mean, where is the line of demarcation? We cover all the news don't we?"

Early on, this kind of question would always leave me with a considerable amount of stress trying to figure out an appropriate response. But later, I began to understand that these vestiges of racism were so deeply rooted and concealed in our everyday activities until any attempt at elucidating the situation made it murkier.

Some examples to wit: New York Times correspondent Richard D. Lyons reported, September 23, 1976 that then Vice President Nelson Rockefeller and House Speaker Carl Albert had engaged in some inappropriate racial comments about Senator Edward Brooke. The remarks were made while the two officials remained unaware that the dais microphones were opened.

The occasion was the visit of Liberian President Dr. William R. Tolbert, representing the first time in the history of the United States that an African head of state addressed a joint session of our congress. This chatter took place as Senator Brooke was serving as a one-man committee to greet and introduce the head of state of an allied nation; one of several incongruities involved here. The other, as Mr. Lyons mentioned in the article, was the conspicuous absence of many Senators and Representatives who had sent their aides to greet a Head-Of-State instead of coming themselves.

The comment drawing the most fire and evoking an apology from House Speaker Albert was his reference to Senator Brooke: "Yeah, he'd be a slave if he were over there." (laughter) In his coverage Richard Lyons pointed out that there are rules prohibiting filming and recording of private conversations among House Members except by consent of the members. Then he went on to reference the National Black Network as one of two news coverage systems that decided to "treat the remarks as news." There in lies the rub. To some, depending on their social views, the microphones being mistakenly left open was the news story. At NBN we disagreed , there should never be a moment so private as to free the two chief officers of our national lawmaking system to muse racist with impunity, open microphones notwithstanding.

A similar note involves the venerable ShowBiz Newspaper, Variety. NBN urged the League of Women Voters to make sure the debates between presidential candidates Gerald Ford and Jimmy Carter included some of the issues of major importance to Black Americans. In so doing, we also offered our facilities as a headquarters for the debates. Variety characterized NBN's " invitation as much of a cry for attention as anything else." This was also in 1976. My retort then probably fits the occasion today as well: " Maybe! But isn't that what our business is about; getting their attention and providing the information they need.

Continuing efforts to get set for the Republican convention initial contact with the Republican National Committee in Washington, D.C. was somewhat awkward. Upon first contact, we were reminded that the Senate Press Gallery was responsible for allocation of media coverage space. We knew that! And I think they knew we knew that.

Now, this is where our game playing would begin. But, we wanted the hierarchy at the Republican Headquarters to know that there was now a Black network on the scene. And our mission was to make sure Blacks had available to them every detail of the convention's activities. So, they played along but never retreated from their position that we must go through the normal procedure.

Basically, the problem with Republicans was the same as with the Democrats. That is we did not, in their view, qualify for a sky suite from which to conduct our broadcasts. They also thought 30 credentials for staff to enter the main arena was an excessive number. The story was very much the same. Namely, we could not get network recognition because the real networks had already claimed the necessary space to provide coverage for the entire nation.

So, how do we break this impasse? We, unfortunately, did not have the contact with influential people in the Republican Party as we had with the Democrats. But we kept working, looking for the slightest opening through which we could push the request.

I am not sure how we decided to seek out the nation's most popular, if not the most powerful, Black Republican. I do remember getting a phone call from Eugene Jackson, instructing me to prepare for a visit to Arthur Fletcher's office in

96

Washington, D.C. I had not met Art but was sharply aware of his image in National government circles.

Based on what I knew of Art, I concluded that this guy must be very bright and skillful. He had parlayed his political achievements to become the first Black Republican cabinet member since the turn of the century. Art Fletcher was appointed to serve as Secretary of Labor by President Richard Nixon.

The incongruity that made the Art Fletcher profile more than ironically exciting was his pragmatic visions on solving America's race problems. Mr. Fletcher, single-handedly conceived, developed and fought like hell for the Philadelphia Plan. It was the Federal Government's first set-aside program. A concept that found its roots under a Republican regime, but later looked upon as dreaded quotas and reversed discrimination by members of both parties.

Back then, the Nixon Administration's "Black Capitalism" program meshed with Art's visions and created a climate in which African American Entrepreneurs could borrow sufficient amounts of business capital. Sufficient, being the keyword here. It was an exceptional time for media firms developed by African Americans. Among them: Earl Graves, (Black Enterprise Magazine) Percy Sutton, (InnerCity Broadcasting) Clarence Smith and Edward Lewis (Essence Magazine) and of course Eugene Jackson and Sydney Small, (owners of the National Black Network).

John Johnson of Ebony and Jet Magazines fame had already made his millions without the Nixon programs. However, for that day and time, Black Businesses had never seen it so good as during "Tricky Dick's" administration. The nickname was pinned to the beleaguered President as he fought impeachment for his role in the Watergate Scandal.

Art Fletcher was more of my kind of man than I had envisioned. Both of his feet were squarely on the ground. We had breakfast with him after leaving his office. The profundity of his scholarship is graciously camouflaged by his folksy sense of humor. As we sat at meat and bread, he assured Gene and me that he understood the problem.

I pondered the prospects: "what exactly does this guy think he can do?" But, then he dispelled my pessimism when he admitted: "this will not be easy." I was overwhelmingly impressed when he vowed not to leave us before some reasonable resolve was met.

The Honorable Mr. Art Fletcher did just that. We must have visited four to five different offices during the course of a full day in the nation's capitol. Art kept Gene and me in tow until finally there was that consensus we were looking for; arrangements for the National Black Network to use a sky-suite as its operations base to cover the Republican National Convention in Kansas City, Missouri.

As all cities do when they are chosen to host either the Olympics or one of the political conventions, Kansas City spared no resources. The next step for us was a prep trip to Kansas City. I had not been there before but this would be the second political convention to our credit. So, we had some very educated notions about where all the broadcast consoles and sundry equipment would likely fit. Provided somebody led us to our space in the arena.

Therefore, to get to that point, we hastily began making trips to the city known the world over for its Barbecued Pork Ribs. (thanks to the New York Times) Just between you, me and the gate post, I had tasted better in Florida as a kid.

Our lead group consisted of Mr. Eddy Hogan-Bassey, director of engineering, Mr. Winston Taylor, one of the staff engineers, Mr. Joe Brown, The Tape ops manager and me. The first trip to Kansas City was an eye opener for me in more than just a few ways. It is already the middle of 1976 and I had been installed as the top man for network operations since the Fall of 1973. The truth is, I was having so much fun making it happen, I never took time to ask; "how am I doing ?"

At this point, I had not been assigned supervisory responsibility in the engineering department. This was Eddy Hogan-Bassey's bailiwick.

Eddy was one of our international celebrities. His brother was the renowned prizefighter, Kid Hogan-Bassey of Lagos, Nigeria. Oddly enough, Winston Taylor, the engineer Eddy called on for special assignment more often than others, was also a celebrity from Africa. Taylor was a superstar soccer player in his homeland of Liberia.

We had a brief layover in Chicago on the way to Kansas City and all four of us deplaned for some Chicago air. With my having recently moved to New York from Chicago, the airport seminar on the pros and cons of Chicago living, was led by me.

As we re-entered the plane, some of the guys were holding cans of soda. (known as "pop" in Chicago) Immediately upon seeing the soda, I stated rather casually that I wish I had known they were going for sodas. Hogan-Bassey abruptly replied that he would get off the plane again for my soda. I pleaded with him briefly, pointing out that the plane was on the verge of takeoff.

I was somewhat amused when he got off the plane but thoroughly perplexed when the craft moved away from the gangway without Eddy. I pondered why . . . why did this man get off the plane on a simple suggestion that I was thirsty? However, after a few air-miles we resigned ourselves to the prospect of his catching the next flight out. We did not see Eddy until the following day.

Nonetheless, my bewilderment over this incident was haunting me as we all went about our individual tasks. There was this sustained vision of Eddy leaving the plane to fetch a soda for a colleague of similar rank in the company. At the basis of my discontent was what exactly did I say to prompt this reaction.

Was he sucking up? Had he accorded clout to my position with the company that I had not yet gleaned. A more dismal analysis would be to find this act indicative of his capacity for leadership. That, however, was out of my jurisdictional reach but this notion commanded a considerable amount of my concern. For this too could be an area for some aggression toward takeover.

As time would eventually prove, I had not taken time to closely evaluate how other persons in the News and Engineering departments regarded my pushy style of getting things done. No one had ever accused me of being particularly cunning nor had I ever thought of myself as being skilled in work-related politics.

It took only two days after the convention got started for the Eddy Hogan-Bassey Spectre to unfortunately raise its head again. He complained to Joe Brown that I had particularly placed him in an inadequate hotel room. This, after I had been so careful to assign him to one of the hotels where all units were suites instead of single rooms. During a brief discussion of the matter, in my usual insensitive manner, I threw fuel onto the fire. Eddy wanted a larger suite for a cocktail party. I abruptly reminded him that our mission was convention coverage and not cocktail sipping. He acknowledged my point of view but left standing his request for a larger suite.

Meanwhile, Joe Brown assisted in arranging for another room. We were happily over the hurdle and Mr. Hogan-Bassey had his cocktail party. I was among the few people who showed up for the affair. The original quarters would have been more than adequate for the number of persons in attendance.

Overall, convention coverage was going well. The usual number of glitches were handled with the appropriate degree of dispatch. But, toward the end of the second day the air was again perforated by the rancid odor of bad interpersonal relations. This time it was serious. I later learned that I had come very close to a full confrontation of mutiny.

I had posted a schedule asking all staff to be at the broadcast location no later than one hour before airtime. I noted no opposition at the time of notification which was posted just as the convention got started. Again, somebody in the group decided I was way off base. All the while, I am assuming all parties involved understood and supported the necessity of being absolutely prepared for a nationwide broadcast.

Developments of the situation unfolded thusly: Eugene Jackson, President of the company, came to Kansas City from New York City and met with the crew before seeing me. This meeting also included my assistant, Joe Brown, who on many occasions found himself on opposite sides of issues involving my directives. In most cases, however, Joe and I could work out our differences of opinion.

100

This one was sort of on the unusual side in that he had not told me of his discontent. I became vaguely aware of the meeting when Joe asked me if Gene had contacted me for a meeting. Which, apparently, was to take place subsequent to their session. There were some conspicuous expressions of disappointment to learn that Gene had not gotten around to rapping my knuckles for being a tyrant. Nonetheless, I continued asking for the best they could give in terms of work performance.

For, in my mind this truly was an historic moment in the annals of African American Journalism. That, of course, was only one side of the equation. I was also propelled by a torrent of selfishness. Albeit in the highest degree of fairness I could muster, I rarely took the low side with regard to the quality of a broadcast. This was finally my moment in the Sun and nobody . . . I mean nobody would blow it for me. Therefore, to ensure that none of the staff members would drop the ball either inadvertently or otherwise, I stayed on the job. Closely involved with every broadcast from the first words ebulliently spoken in the morning to the weary whisper of the final words in the evening.

So, just as Joe had warned . . . Gene Jackson did catch up with me and invited me to breakfast as well. He was very respectful in spelling out that it was a consensus among the brass that I operated with a heavy hand and he didn't think it was necessary.

I acknowledged his reprimand but not without offering up a minor defense for my position on the matter. Particularly the situation that brought about this bit of disunity in the first place. I began by asking if he thought it was heavy handed to require staff in position one hour before the broadcast as do the big networks.

Then I continued explaining that in order to make sure all hands were in place on time, as I left the pool side to take a shower, I reminded them of the reporting time. And invariably, several of them would be still at poolside as I passed again, on the way to the one rental car available to us.

101

On this day in question, one of them yelled out for me to wait until they all showered. I advised them to take a cab. I concluded that's when certain of the staff thought it necessary to call Home Office. At the end of my dissertation, Gene did assuage my troubled heart somewhat by saying he understood. Conversely, he thought there was room for a softer approach. Coverage of the GOP convention went well and we recorded another milestone for NBN.

12

The gentle hands of time cradled us and continued pushing us on to bigger and better things. We were, as anybody could see growing in spite of ourselves. Somewhere along the way somebody acknowledged that we were a network of all male voices; nary a female on the air. In short order, efforts were afloat to correct this "politically incorrect" situation.

Our first female voice came in a rather sizable package. Claudia Polley's, silky sounding voice was noticeably soft when she spoke casually . . . but not when she approached that microphone to deliver a newscast. Ms. Polley stood at least six feet two inches tall with a very good-to-look-at face. She was a talented broadcaster with worthy experience and restless ambitions.

The author never witnessed any demonstrations in support of her claims to being a concert singer, but her resume boastfully stipulated extensive work at Julliard School of Music in New York City.

One thing for sure, Claudia held her own among the other anchors on the staff. On more than one occasion, she was observed in hot debate, fending off two and three of the guys in the newsroom simultaneously. The repartee was replete with language somewhat out of range for usage in a newscast but typical of newsroom chatter. So, in a virtual sense Claudia was one of the guys. They treated her that way and she responded in kind.

Claudia Polley's stay with NBN was short lived. It was as if her appointed mission was to serve as the first female announcer for the network and move on to otherwise unrelated endeavors. And, that is what she did. As we understood it at the time of her resignation, Claudia would take a job with the city administration in Pritchard, Alabama.

Nevertheless, we remembered Claudia not only as the first lady of the NBN airwaves; but an outstanding contributor to the early development of the network. However, long after her departure, she was quoted as having found those days at NBN stifling. Ms. Polley moved around quite frequently. It was said she was one of those who led the fight to allow women reporters into professional sports locker rooms.

The next female voice acquired by the network was more of "the joke's on you Big Boy" than anything I can remember associated with NBN. When I first heard the audition tape of Ricki Stevenson, it was like listening to a beloved melody, cherishing the crescendos while caressing the diminuendos and the pregnant pauses as well. Ricki had a natural ability to make a piece of news copy sound like something you had been waiting all day to hear. Her voice was just right; not too much of a girl sound and nowhere near a male sound. And, whoever trained her, taught her how to punch it when needed and pause it, when it works.

As I begun to inquire about her, I was told of her feeding stories to the Network on occasions through our affiliate in Nashville, Tennessee. The pressure from front office had been mounting by the seconds. In the words of Gene Jackson: "And, she's got to be the best out there." Then he would name every biggy at the major networks who happens to be black and female and instruct me to call them and offer them jobs at NBN.

And, of course, it was my job to say okay and ask myself . . . "for what?" Gene would always tell me to go out and get the best, no matter what the cost. But by the time the project got to Sydney there would be no budget for it.

What we all agreed on, however, finding a good female voice was the first order of business, now that we had lost Claudia Polley. In my mind . . . this woman was Ricki Stevenson. I had decided that from the first moment I heard her tape.

While pondering this matter, my deductions led me to believe at first that it would probably be difficult to lure her from her current job. That is if they saw in her what I thought I heard in her. Nevertheless, she was the sound I felt the network needed and that's what we are going to do.

So, I called Ms. Stevenson. At first, it appeared Ricki could not reconcile the possibility of getting a job offer from the tape she had mailed across the nation. She was very indifferent and skeptical of my initial call. So much so that I became impatient after a conversation that lasted no fewer than five minutes. Throughout the entire phone conversation, she did everything she could to avoid admitting that she sent out the tape in search of employment.

I found her skilled at ducking the central focus of any question she felt the need not to answer. What I failed to understand was why she was being so evasive during a job interview. The surprising answer to that question came during the subsequent phone conversation. She did not believe it was a job interview. It apparently was one of those situations where: "I'll ask the world for something and figure out what to do with it when it comes."

Before hanging up the phone in a state of mild disappointment, I firmly reiterated my desire to continue talking to her about a News Anchor position with NBN and instructed her to call me when she could discuss the subject more freely. I waited two weeks and no phone call from Ricki Stevenson. Now I have another problem. How do I resume these talks without giving her the impression that she represents an element the network must have at any cost?

In order to get on with my career, namely, the building of a network...I made the call. When she answered the phone, Ms. Stevenson confessed: 1) She thought I was conducting some sort of hoax 2) She might not be ready to go chasing around the country working for people she did not know. Bingo! There it is; this is a kid trying to show off some sophistication she doesn't have. Subsequent revelations: 1) Just out of College. 2) Working at the affiliated station was her first full time job. Now the table is turned, I now need more time to think over these new discoveries: "I really would like to have her sound on the network. However, I don't know if I can cope with this other baggage."

With the next phone conversation considerable progress was realized. I made her a firm offer and asked her to keep me abreast of her plans to give proper notice to her present employer. This is an area where extreme caution was recommended because we did not want to generate any bad relationships with our affiliates by pirating their staff members. After going into some details about her duties and rate of pay, I was sure we were on our way and she would be calling soon to make final arrangements.

There were two more calls from Ricki Stevenson but the first was to tell me that she would not be joining us. When asked why, she informed me of a conversation between she and her mother which led to that decision. None of what she explained made any sense, but at that point I had had it. And, wished her the best with her broadcast career.

Just as I thought the discussion was over her voice squeaked like I had never heard it before . . . "I don't know how to write a newscast . . . I've never written one in my life."

In an effort to allay some of the anxiety I heard in her expressions . . . I assured her that most of us had to be trained to write for a network. But, she said . . . "I don't have to write stories here, all we do is take them from the wire service and read them." And, my inquiry as to whether she had through her own initiative written local interest stories was met with an emphatic, NO! She waited for me to respond . . . it took a few seconds before I got the courage to say . . . "I will personally teach you the technique of writing for the network." I figured this was a no-brainer; she is a college grad.

Ricki Stevenson finally became a member of the NBN on-air staff. Within six months she was complaining about the kind of news we chose to cover. Declaring that we were no more of a benefit to the black population than the already established radio news networks. She became a full fledge in-house activist. In her second year with the company, Ricki led the movement to further unionize the network thereby being at the forefront of the company's second labor union strike.

Most of us in management knew the broadcast division would inevitably become fully unionized. But, I had to personally come to grips psychologically with the pros and cons of a high profile strike against this rare animal called "Black Owned and Operated Radio Network." It gets more entangled than some of us are willing to acknowledge. I agreed the staffers, under the influence of perceived denial by ownership, had a right to ask for raises. Tied to that is the other misguided notion "how dare you treat us this way; the National Black Network is suppose to represent at least a partial remedy to my being the last hired and the first fired, and systematically underpaid by the establishment."

Ask for raises, OK, but walking out should have been closely and deeply examined as an option toward a solution. The Network was never the same. But, life is never the same from day to day. There were some deep scars left. Some of my better talents walked out an never returned. As in every strike that persist beyond three weeks, the workers suffer most.

As for Gene and Syd's response to this bit of our history, they did foresee the pain forthcoming in the network's growth. However, they appeared to be standing on a principle: "It is our company and we will defend our right to make a profit in addition to paying you a fair wage." By the same measures, just because the ownership is Black, it would have been fiscally irresponsible to encourage workers to organize against the company.

There was baggage on both sides. For whatever it is worth, there was an assertive move on the part of ownership to work out an in-house type of committee to handle grievances. We sought this course of action after learning that there was a consensus among staff aimed at organizing a union.

However, I am not 100% sure we selected the best available strategy. Gene and Syd sent Del Raycee, the white guy, to talk over this highly sensitive issue with some young black guys, who felt they were being inappropriately treated by some more privileged black guys. But this was not the only time Del had been sent to perform tasks that did not, under the circumstances, fit his persona nor his portfolio. But, then again, that's what all of this is about . . . confusion engendered by the fallout of racism. For without racism and other socio-political issues, there would not have been a need for a "Black" radio network.

From the operations manual of the streets comes this admonition: "when in doubt, punt." Very often, when it was obvious that Gene and Syd were unsure about what the next step should be, they would send Del. It might be worth adding also that these were the areas in which Del was the most vulnerable. He welcomed all challenges of intrigue. Gene and Syd would throw up the smoke screen and Del delighted in the development of strategies and schemes to dispel the entangled.

The above mentioned labor union organizing activities at NBN resulted in a hodgepodge of representation that no other radio network in the nation would tolerate. NBN's announcers became members of the National Association of Broadcast Electricians and Technicians (NABET). For more than a half century, the conventional union for announcers had been the American Federation of Television and Radio Artists (AFTRA).

It was extremely difficult to counteract the movement. In those days, before president Ronald Regan attempted to modify the awesome clout enjoyed by organized labor, it was far more "politically incorrect" to appear anti-labor than to be against the civil rights movement. All of this however, was a tremendous learning experience for those of us intrinsically involved in a start-up media corporation. Ours was truly a unique culture within the not so ordinary culture of the broadcast industry.

The fallout factors of this relationship with its built-in animus was sometimes damaging to certain employees. The union introduced a new look and feel for an otherwise amiable atmosphere; one in which the freedom to befriend above and below your working rank was normal.

So, when all of the factors are examined such as labor union zealots and those wretched souls who seemed doomed to screwing up plus the realities of my personality... a boss who did not leave much room for poor performance or behavioral improprieties, things were tough. The overall atmosphere in our newsroom and studios was fraught with varying degrees of tension.

One of those who suffered a significant loss during this stage of the network's development was a youngster named Erwin Cochran. Mr. Cochran was quite young when he came to us with extremely limited experience. At age 21 he had been working for a local radio station in the nearby state of Connecticut.

Roy West and I met with Mr. Cochran, expressed our desire to help him with his development as a newsman and emphasized that continued growth would be required in order to keep his job. We started him out on the graveyard shift.

It was only a short while until Mr. Cochran became a full supporter of the union organizing activities. And at some point, the nice humble gentleman we had promised an opportunity to further his broadcasting skills, set aside that aspect of his personality to join the undiscriminating group mostly responsible for composing the union's rhetoric. The union organizers pounced on his lack of sophistication and made him the point man.

NABET (National Association of Broadcast Electricians & Technicians)was trying to invade the traditional turf of AFTRA (American Federation of Radio and Television Artists) by organizing announcers at NBN in addition to the operating engineers. Throughout the industry NABET was known as the engineers union and AFTRA the union for announcers and other on-air performers. But what better scenario for a hostile intrusion through these traditional turf lines than at a fledgling minority network where resources were at best limited. I personally perceived that they couldn't have gotten away with this at NBC, ABC, CBS or MUTUAL. So, I took a stand.

It was unlawful for me to attempt to tell the staff that they were being used as pawns in a turf war. And that there were racial aspects to the overall picture... using the new Black network as a guinea pig in the union's campaign to expand from a technical union to a talent union. The staff members, of course would have had scarce grounds on which to accept my premise; in their minds I was the primary enemy and was trying to prevent the organizing process.

Shortly after AFTRA all but abandoned its campaign to block the NABET initiative, NBN management began preparing for the new arrangement. Subsequently, NABET took over full control of the NBN shop and I wasn't happy about it but gave the new order my full cooperation.

In months to follow, I would use Erwin Cochran to demonstrate my point. Why? Because he was the weakest journalist on the staff. And as I sat in my office seconds after hearing his outburst in the newsroom next door threatening to close the doors if the NABET ratification didn't take place, I knew I had to engineer his displacement. But, moreover, this would be very important to the operations of the network. For decades . . . broadcast entities in America have fought to maintain unencumbered rights to replace talent whenever necessary. Talent is the lifeblood of Television and Radio. Talent is at the very heartbeat of the broadcast industry's commerce.

I would fight in that tradition.

Several months later a very controversial movie came to the forefront when the NAACP took issue with the makers of the film. It was entitled "White Dog." The story line was about a big white dog trained to attack black persons on first sight. The NAACP leadership denounced the film as incredibly damaging. Other responsible observers of the media joined in and raised vociferous objections to release of the movie.

The script moved on to the eventuality of the dog falling under the influence of a young white woman who was blind. The producers found some solace in the extraordinary effort on her part to teach the "White Dog" not to hate Black Human Beings.

But the voices of opposition were not at all assuaged by this development as a remedy to this wretched story line. They remained enraged over the thought that someone would purposely teach a dog to choose his prey based on race or skin color. A perplexing news story to say the least but major media were careful not to give it too much front page exposure. But, this is what a Black network was created for!

While all of this hovered overhead I envisioned my ugly agenda. Immediately, I saw it as an opportunity to allow Mr. Cochran to prove his journalistic worth. Though, I had not seen any evidence of his having neither the experience nor the basic skills to ferret out all of the crucial components of this (such a sensitive) story.

Nonetheless, my office was mandated under both the company brass and the union hierarchy to mete out assignments

110

and awards on an equitable basis. Therefore, it was my obligatory option, according to the union contract, to assign Mr. Cochran to the story whether I thought he could proficiently perform the task or not.

When I handed the story assignment to Erwin Cochran, there was an overt look of vagueness on his face. He took the memo in hand and went back to his desk with little more to say than thank you. A week went by and no report was forwarded on the various elements on which I had instructed him.

A subsequent deadline for review was set and not met. At that point, I began filing away documents on each of our discussions. Most of them demonstrated his failure to keep pace on the development of the project. The fact that the air date for the half-hour special had been postponed due to his tardiness was also put to paper and filed.

Following a brief period of him trying to convince me that I had overvalued the story, Cochran was warned that he was extremely close to the brink of insubordination. His notion was somewhat based on his telephone interview with the renowned, but mostly unemployed during those days, actor Paul Winfield.

Mr. Winfield had a lead role in "White Dog" and assured Mr. Cochran that he had solid grounds for disagreeing with the NAACP's interpretation of its content. In summary, Cochran did not finish the story and I fired him based on insubordination provisions in the NABET union contract.

A considerable amount of heat was generated for placing the company in such a state of risk with the union. But, this was one of those occasions when I had Syd Small as an ally. He and I knew for certain that the union would fight this one to the dregs of its resources. It happened just that way. The arbitration sessions persisted for exactly two years.

I was told that Cochran never sought employment elsewhere because he was convinced the union would keep its promise and see that he was never ever fired. And, upon his victory he would receive a lump sum of cash as restitution plus a recall to his job.

We won the case and Erwin Cochran went on his dejected way. The last time I saw him, he appeared to be doing quite well singing at weddings. He did always fancy himself a rather gifted

111

singer. This was most unfortunate but I needed to put the union on notice that we would not rollover and play dead while it used NBN (the new kid on broadcast row) as a test rabbit.

The Cochran case provided some moments of wrenching anxiety with highs and lows to both extremes. Del Raycee worked with me on building the defense under the legal tutelage of John Somers. He was chief counsel for NBN from day one. That topic alone is worthy of a book. He was the other white guy I failed to mention in the earlier chapters herewith.

During one of the sessions, lawyers for the union spent an inordinate amount of time trying to persuade the arbitrator that I had made a big deal of a story that most other media had not seen fit to even cover at all. On that very same day the arbitrator carried underneath his arm a New York City newspaper with the story on the front page.

Del Raycee, who was at his best in this kind of situation, called the newspaper to my attention. The arbitrator carried it under his arm as he stood in the men's room relieving himself. Del then indicated that we should skirt the rules a bit by making certain the arbitrator took special note of the "front page" position of the "White Dog" story.

I was reluctant as we began leaning closer to each other, shoulder-to-shoulder, talking just above a whisper. At that moment, I could see a wry looking smirk on Del's face…I knew it was only a matter of time. He couldn't resist it! This was his kind of party!

It would have been too much conformity for Del to wait until after the recess and try to introduce it as evidence in support of our defense. Del always needed the excitement of having the edge. This was the edge! Bring supportive evidence to the judge's attention while he is trying to take a leak. And do it now! Do it without discussing it with your lawyer who is just outside the door in a room across the hall.

Del, with his usual impetuosity, mentioned it. The Judge was kind. He did not reprimand Del as he very well could have. Instead, he shrugged off Del's aggressiveness without any indication of whether we had scored or had not. At that point we had no way of knowing if this risky crap roll by Del had lost the case for us or otherwise.

Nevertheless, Del and I walked out of the men's room giggling with glee as if we had already won the case. Little did we know that it would take more than a year longer to finally have the judge rule in our favor. The union did not go away and none of us expected it to.

13

I had heard the name Warren Dean on several occasions while talking about the various black talents at other networks and stations. But, I had never bothered to listened to him over at ABC until one of the guys in our shop urged me to listen, explaining that he was quite good. I did and was really impressed with what I heard. I asked the guys to let Warren know that I wanted to meet him.

Before he and I got to meet, the NBN staffers were bandying about a barrage of accolades for the management over at ABC. This was the one network that was blazing a trail worthy of note. They were blanketing the nation with no fewer than four separate networks; each requiring a specific style of writing and vocal delivery. Most of this admiration from the discussion was directed at the tough-minded broadcast executive over there named, Tom O'Brien.

Tom was a hero of sorts. Many of the people who had worked under Tom talked about him with considerable respect and apprehension at the same time. According to them, to fear Tom and his toughness was alright. Along with working for Tom comes the profile of having sufficiently met a standard of matriculation.

This was the Warren Dean connection. My guys were impressed with Dean. For his skills were at a level worthy of remaining under the auspices of Tom O'Brien. The one surprise in meeting Warren, eventually, was his somewhat immodest expressions about his success in network radio.

He graciously came to see me after I let out the word that I would like to meet him. His full name is Warren Dean Schomburg, a direct descendent of famous historian, Arturo Schomburg. Arturo founded the renowned Schomburg Museum of African History and Culture, an institution one must not miss when visiting Harlem, New York. Warren is a Grandson to the late Arturo Schomburg.

On the day he entered my office, Warren did a quick left-to-right with his entire head instead of his eyes. In that moment, I could tell he had surveyed the room from wall-to-wall as though he was following the volley of a tennis match. The three straight chairs lined on the wall less than five feet from my metallic desk were easily accessible as he slid into the second one. He appeared a little unsure about what was to take place . . . but it didn't bother him much.

I got started abruptly; telling him that I had been listening to his newscasts and was extremely impressed. He was gracious, although he didn't seem surprised. After he thanked me, I moved on to further explanations on why I thought this meeting was necessary.

All went well until I got to the part where I suggested that there may come a day when he could possibly consider coming to work for the National Black Network. And, I alluded that this conclusion could be based on some of the sentiments that brought me back; being tired of getting kicked around by the adversary.

It was as if I had stepped on his toe wearing football cleats. Although, I could see the indignation deeply furrowed in his brow, Warren restrained himself and never raised his voice. Nevertheless, the words of his indictment were stinging and oh so familiar for that day and time:

"Why are Blacks so quick to conclude that other Blacks cannot achieve based on merit . . .as opposed to some form of benevolence on the part of the white man?"

I thought to myself, "if only he knew that not only am I an ally of Warren Dean, I am a fan." Then he followed with an admonition sure to put me in my place: "My new contract which is due for renewal soon, will raise my gross income to 45 thousand dollars a year, I doubt you guys will be able to match that."

Of course, I had to concede his observation. However, I could not leave our conversation there. I felt the need to share with him some of the wisdom hard gained through experiences that I could not have foreseen either. I explained that I had just been released from a contract at NBC right on the heels of

116

winning awards and commendation letters from the brass at headquarters. Then, in an attempt to put the black journalist's role in perspective, I related these facts:

"I was recruited by NBC to fill a slot that had been held by a Black before my arrival. And I was replaced by a black female. Subsequently, she was replaced by a Black man. This is pretty much the pattern you will find throughout the industry."

Needless to say, Warren departed my office carrying less than a great degree of fondness for Vince Sanders, I am sure. But to his credit, Warren was always a gentleman. And, over the years as I got to know him better, he substantiated his hereditary pedigree. But, as fate would have it, that initial visit to my office would not be his last one.

The contract renewal that Warren had wholeheartedly anticipated would raise his annual income to 45K, did not materialize, nor was it as negotiable as he had first thought. But, this was not a rare occurrence it seems. There were standing industry jokes about being employed at ABC. It was said that many staffers, particularly those on-air, lived in a perpetual state of tenuity. The joke was that many of them were even afraid to take earned vacation for fear of returning to a pink slip. As we all know, the talent end of broadcasting is migratory at best, ethnic background or skin color, notwithstanding.

I never learned exactly why O'Brien did not retain the services of Warren Dean. History continued writing itself in the NBN newsroom and several months down the road, I received a phone call from Warren. Being the proud fellow he is, Warren will only eat but so much crow. I picked up the phone and said: "Hello?" A very crisp voice responded saying: "Hello Vince, did your boss speak to you? I paused...and seemed to recall moaning a little before my state of surprise freed me to ask: "who'? "Mr. Eugene Jackson." Did he speak to you? "Well . . . no . . . about what?" Then it fell on my ears like a cascade of sour notes from the vocal chords of Tiny Tim: " I am not going to renew my contract with ABC and Mr. Jackson said I should talk to you about joining the National Black Network."

I was both amused and somewhat disturbed at the same time. It took a moment to reconcile the full picture of what was taking place. Then, I became a bit empathetic and realized that I too probably would have sought to cover my head in the same manner. Without further ado, he was amicably granted a meeting. And much to my delight, before the meeting got started, Warren underscored his true character by offering an unsolicited apology for some of the shortsighted comments made during our first meeting.

It was either the next day or the following that Gene would call and attempt to prepare me for a phone call I had already fielded. He and I chuckled over the irony and complexities spawned by the various forms of racial fallout. We ended our chat with a repetition of the long-standing query of when will they go away; the delusions inherent in our perceptions that we can achieve by simply meeting the performance standards set by the adversary. As he concluded the phone conversation, Gene reminded me that he and I were obligated to assure Warren that he, in fact, did get to ABC on his merit, despite what happened in the aftermath.

Now comes the unfortunate moment of truth about this episode involving Warren Dean and NBN. He worked for the network for quite a few flawless years. In addition to his stellar on-air work, Mr. Dean offered some noteworthy creative input to the overall scheme of things.

However, on this one occasion, as it was related to me by Art Whaley, who was in charge of the newsroom at the time, Warren either could not locate his favorite typewriter or could not get it to function properly. Based on this perceived administrative deficiency, he failed to select another typewriter in the room and did not prepare a newscast at all.

Therefore, the network was blank all over the nation for that hour. When Art Whaley called me to inform me of the unfortunate incident, it took all of 30 seconds to ask each other: "why?"...and consequently decide that it was an infraction that dictated the ultimate in punitive measures.

14

After we got used to being able to operate and pay the bills in New York's proverbial high-rent district, things kept getting better. One of the most rewarding sequences for yours truly was the experience that brought me into close contact with two of the nation's true icons of the theater, Ossie Davis and his wife Ruby Dee.

I am not sure how they got hooked up with us but it is one fascinating story, to say the least. First off, if anybody had said to me back then when newsrooms were living by the almighty "10-second sound bite" and "talk radio" was an unforgivable interruption of the disco music sound, we want these two actors to read stories and poetry on the radio…"yeah right!" But, that's just what it was . . . the Ossie Davis and Ruby Dee Story Hour.

A one hour radio show during which Ossie and Ruby would do nothing other than tell folk tales and read poetry and believe me, for those of you who did not hear the show, you missed an opportunity to hear real talent at work. Moreover, you missed a superior demonstration of the ultimate power of the spoken word; the handing down of knowledge through the auditory faculties alone.

The initial information I received on the Story Hour came from Chicago. I was more than a little bit surprised when my secretary announced that Barbara Proctor of the famed Proctor and Gardner Advertising Agency was calling to speak to me. I had known Barbara from the days when she worked at several other advertising agencies in Chicago. A brief but enriching span of our relationship brought together my singing group in her luxury apartment on Sunday afternoons. She would write commercial copy samples and along with the music director of the group, Mr. Delano O'Bannion, lay the tracks with piano music to a hand-held cassette recorder. It was never clear what she would do with those pieces on Monday morning. A safe bet is that this was the only way she could get a shot at eventually becoming a full-fledged producer of radio commercials;

composing and recording them at home and handing them off to some benefactor at the job.

Nonetheless, Barbara Proctor would go on to make her mark on the advertising agency world and subsequently use the National Black Network as one of her major broadcast media allies. My early contact with her was in the late 50's, clearly a few years before African Americans would influence the content of radio commercials intended for their consumption. The earlier reference to the singing group as mine was a misappropriation of the facts. The group was a fine arts singing group, formed by Mr. Delano O'Bannion, a world class "basso profundo."

O'Bannion had succeeded in convincing about ten alumnae of Fisk University to help him carry on the unparalleled musical traditions established at Fisk University by Professor John W. Work. Thus, the group was known as the "The John W. Work Chorale." I called it my group because I was the chorale's manager and preformed with it as a dramatic narrator.

In 1963 , the great Duke Ellington, took the Chorale to Brazil to perform with his orchestra at the World Music Festival. Another familiar name who made that trip was actor Lou Gossett, Jr. known for his work as a folk singer back in those days.

Meanwhile, back to Barbara's call to me at the Network. She complained in a very inarticulate manner about some young impudent salesman from the network named Syd Small. Ms. Proctor was convinced that this man knew nothing about protocol and was only inches from blowing the deal that she and her staff had worked so diligently to make happen.

Her reference was to the tentative arrangements securing Kraft Foods as an exclusive sponsor of the Ossie Davis/ Ruby Dee Story Hour. I was somewhat unprepared for this and Barbara apparently did not know that Syd was my boss and not the other way around.

After urging me to reel in this renegade before he does further damage, Barbara failed miserably in her attempt to explain what rules Sydney had broken. Left with little else from which to choose, I jumped to judgement and concluded that this was a personality clash.

I knew these two individuals. Barbara's ego was saying: "OK fella, I got what you need, a full year sponsorship of your yet unproven radio show...but first you must ask me for it."

Conversely, there was Syd camouflaging a dearth of sophistication with antagonizing silence. So, you've got what we used to call a Mexican Standoff; there is no communication and neither party feels he/she is to blame.

The brightest side of this amusing phone call was that I learned we were on the verge of some major new programming, fully sponsored, nonetheless. For some reason or the other I remained alert enough to avoid telling Barbara that Syd was one of the owners of the company.

Looking back, I was even more alert in my decision not to call Chicago and let Syd know he was perceived as a troublemaker by the advertising executive who was holding a $400,000. contract for the network. So, I found Gene Jackson and carefully inquired as to the whereabouts of Syd. As the conversation continued . . . I gently selected my spot to tell him that our deal with Kraft Foods was facing some possible difficulties.

I have yet to learn the details of what transpired from that point on but the significant part of our history, namely the production of the Ossie Davis/Ruby Dee Story hour, did come to fruition. In the beginning, the show was recorded and edited at some other production facility until somebody remembered the surplus of space and microphones available at the NBN studio.

A plethora of methods were employed to put the show together from time to time. At one point, the stars had their son, Guy Davis, come in and perform live music for the segments of the show. This was fun watching them set moods and select original music for the single segments. Having Guy in the studio was more than just a perfunctory show business gesture. Ossie (King Davis) worked harder in support of a strong family than he did a strong Ossie; if such is possible.

To know Ossie Davis and his wife Ruby Dee is a wonderful odyssey through a celestial state of harmony at all costs. It is no

121

accident that these two are successful actors with healthy bodies, healthy minds, healthy children and among all the most difficult to maintain, a healthy marriage; particularly when both are successful movie stars. With all of the marvelous work these two have done both together and separately, it is no world shattering breakthrough for me to remind you that Ossie Davis and Ruby Dee are VERY special.

I would refer to Ossie as the keystone of his family's success but I am sure he would have a problem with such a narrow perspective. Nonetheless, he is without a doubt the principal factor. His personal carriage is cardinal and it appears the ultimate in strength. The kind of strength that provides a place in which Ruby can cuddle and curl into and know no harm. He would carry her in his arms and never look down at her until she breaks his vigilant concentration with one of her cooing sounds. To see this picture up close leads one to the conclusion that they were Divinely matched; She is a finely tuned instrument and he is a fierce force of precision. I have seen her play to the demand of the occasion. He on the other hand, with every regal step, whether intended or not, demands the utmost in human behavior. People who come to work with Ossie, come to perform at high levels because that is what Ossie Davis represents; high level performances, from start to finish.

Through all of this, he maintains the degree of tenderness needed to enhance the harmony required in the work they do. Ossie always did claim to do his best writing in the early dawn, sometimes rising at 2am while Ruby remained asleep. In that same style, when reporting for his daily appointments, he is invariably 30 minutes to an hour ahead of the schedule. With Ruby, not so. She is always a half hour late.

During our travels throughout the country promoting Story Hour, Ossie would, without fail, be among the first to enter the limo after having spent some time waiting in the hotel lobby. Whenever anyone in the car would inquire about Ruby, he would not offer any form of explanation or apology. On occasions when someone new to the experience asserted even a second inquiry, they too, were greeted with not a mumbling word. Those of us who knew the deal . . . understood that she would be there when she gets there and nobody should raise it as an issue. Every morning, when she got into the limo, she did not offer an excuse or explanation for her tardiness nor did he ask her for one.

I concluded, in my humble claims to a modicum of wisdom, that this must be the secret to their professional success. . . respect and appreciation for your mate's individuality. Based on the tenure involved here, one would hazard a guess that there just might also be some REAL LOVE in this renowned union.

Whatever! It works like a charm for Ossie and Ruby. The story Hour was an amazing success. Who would have believed that in a day when FM radio was knocking AM radio out of the box and filling the early 1970's with radio stations that programmed nothing but wall-to-wall music . . . moving through the ending moments of Motown's magic to the dawning of the deafening disco years, that a couple of mature personalities could attract a listening audience large enough to satisfy an advertiser such as Kraft Foods.

Ah!. . . but there goes the goose with the golden egg. Kraft was looking for the family image in the advertising of its food line. So, does the Ossie Davis/Ruby Dee husband-wife team of actors telling African folk tales and reciting African American poetry fit the bill?...Right On!

Did it work? You bet! The show was in production for three years and we aired reruns for an additional two years. What always amazed me was the way these two advanced actors were always thronged by teenagers as we visited high school campuses around the country. Yes, it did work!

What didn't work for the network, however, was an effort to continue the relationship with Kraft Foods at the same level of advertising without Ossie & Ruby. Somewhere in the circuitry which included our front office, C. Roy Jackson and Barbara Proctor's Advertising Agency, It was decided that the client needed to be in touch with "Today's Black Woman." And, that's what they named the half-hour magazine style program designed to succeed the Story Hour.

Enter Vy Higginson, the quintessential black woman, a big radio name in New York City. If you are wondering whether this is the same Vy Higginson who subsequently became a multimillionaire after writing and producing an off-off Broadway gospel musical called "Mama I wanna Sing" . . . yes! You are absolutely correct . . . same lady. But this fortune was yet to come.

When she came to the studio to record "Today's Black Woman," Vy was accompanied by her former schoolmate, Joyce Griffin. At first, they appeared to be a good team. Joyce was the producer of the show until Vy decided otherwise after a few episodes were taped. Ms. Higginsen, then tried a hand at producing the show while still performing as talent. If ever there was a situation befitting the old adage, "too many cooks spoil the broth" . . . "Today's Black Woman" was the epitome.

It was in keeping with other forms of overkill among Blacks and Whites of goodwill, trying to correct centuries-old problems in all American industries, not just in media. By the same token much of the clamor was opportunistic commercialism, as well. Nonetheless, the media had unique positions and responsibilities.

It was the early seventies, the cities around the country were still smarting from some of the most destructive racial riots the country had ever seen. Fresh in the memory of America's predominantly white political leadership was the penetrating effectiveness of Black Media (mainly radio)in quelling the outbreaks in the cities. With the revelation of these two sleeping giants: one that is capable of serious destruction to the nation's entire infrastructure and the other in a position to cool out that ominous potential, came the acknowledgment of serious omissions.

Primary among them was the fact that the African American consumer had been all but ignored. The assumption was that those who could afford quality product and services could be reached through general media advertising. Therefore, eliminating the need to spend money in Black owned media. This was another area of extreme sensitivity because while radio was the most effective reach into the black community, most of the radio stations were still owned by whites. Thereby adding complications to a clear definition of black media.

So, when the efforts to make amends were undertaken by the ruling class, there was a misguided assumption that all blacks knew what was good for and acceptable to all other blacks . . . wrong! But, how were they to know? Nonetheless, this gave rise to a floodtide of ideas from a wide variety of Blacks listing themselves as consultants. Some proposed talking to the Black Family in a suit and tie in recognition of its dignity. Others built commercials with persons in dashikis and wearing uncontrollably large afro hair styles in sympathy with a nationalistic identity.

Who was going to tell us what should be the contents of "Today's Black Woman?" The advertisers were afraid of taking a chance on possibly offending the very people they wanted to reach. In the case of Kraft Foods, they hired a black lifestyles consultant. His name was C. Roy Jackson, he was working in tandem with the black advertising agency, Proctor & Gardner. It too, by virtue of its exclusive portfolio, was an expert on Black Lifestyles.

Then, of course, there is the National Black Network, most definitely designed to fashion all of its programming for the consumption of Americans of African descent. To meet that objective, it too must have advanced information on the mores of being black in America. Finally, there are the hostess and the producer, two black women, responsible for writing the script and projecting its contents to "Today's Black Woman" all across America.

Trying to put into action a show with the best format for reaching the Black Woman was a tough question even for a contingent of experts such as those available to us. If it were a show about the makeup and beauty applications used by Black Women, that's OK! But that kind of show should never be mistaken as some vehicle to bring about social and political betterment. Nor should these metaphors be allowed to mix as if they carried the same value.

"Today's Black Woman" did not survive the "too many cooks" cross-fertilization. All of the entities involved could not resist trying to make the program a panacea for the cause. This fixation eventually led to a name change. "Today's Black

Woman" became "Action Woman." It died also. The name was much more befitting but the "too many cooks" syndrome had already taken its toll.

But before we finally put it to rest there was an extension of the Chicago Connection aimed at trying to save the project. As I recall the sequence of events, Syd asked if I thought my longtime friend and former co-worker, Merri Dee,(no relations to Ruby Dee) would be interested in doing the show. Merri was a TV personality at WGN in Chicago. I called and she was interested. But the fact remained that talent was not the problem for the show.

Merri Dee was flown in from Chicago to tape the shows. It worked well for a short while. There were several distractions along the way but nothing we couldn't correct. By this time, I had become more personally involved with the in-studio process of the show. On several occasions, I flew out to Chicago and rented studio time for the taping. But it was only a matter of time before we would face reality; It was impossible to cram remedies for all of our social ills into one half hour radio show.

The pressure generated here was based on the fact that a thirty-minute single sponsor show on a radio network was a very rare bird, if you will. And super rare for the only Black network in existence. We could not duplicate the deal we had with Kraft Foods no matter how hard we tried. With several minority owned businesses of a peripheral nature perched on the coattail of this Project, the impact would be heavy in the world of advertising to black audiences. But we all moved on cherishing the better moments generated through the tandem of NBN and Proctor and Gardner Advertising.

Dick Gregory is greeted by "Story Hour" co-host Ruby Dee as he arrives for a guest appearance on the show. The executive producer of "Story Hour", Vince Sanders, joins Ms. Dee in welcoming the veteran Comedian.

Actor Ossie Davis appears otherwise occupied as his wife, actress Ruby Dee, frolics through mounds of fan mail with executive producer Vince Sanders. Ms. Dee and Mr. Davis were co-hosts of the overwhelmingly successful "Story Hour" show.

15

The following is a quote from the world's most renowned peanut farmer: "Mr. Sanders, thank you very much. When I get to the White House, I will remember you... I promise."

It wasn't like clockwork but it did happen. President Jimmy Carter had his staff to call and tell me the National Black Network had been granted an exclusive interview with the President of the United States. This call came about 6 months into his presidency. He made the promise after an interview at the network during his campaign.

Eugene Jackson appeared to understand the significance of this phone call. Immediately, Gene was on the phone soliciting advertising. He got Sears to sponsor the entire thirty minutes. Right away I began wondering if others in the office were taking note. We all knew it wasn't easy but the more you shake the trees the greater the probability some fruit will fall. And the advertisers will advertise and we will have a stronger platform from which to pitch the stations for clearance.

Admittedly, this is simpler said than done. In spite of the struggle to demonstrate value in good market-related programming, there were also other strides that gave us the appearance of a progressive communications company. Early in its existence, Unity Broadcasting held a significant investor's position in the first cellular phone project in Detroit. It later applied, in partnership with InnerCity Broadcasting, for the cable franchise in Queens County, NY; two ventures that netted appreciable achievement and wealth for Syd and Gene..

Then came the purchase of three radio stations. This registered as a good business move except for the problems encountered in St. Louis. There the company bought what had been known as the premiere black station in the city and failed to turn it around. Unfortunately, the company did not have a flow chart that afforded it the capacity to operate a division that far away from headquarters.

Conversely, the station in Philadelphia, which was already printing its own money, so to speak, and located a short train ride away, was a remarkable success story. But not enough to unify ownership to greater heights. Before Gene took the Philadelphia property in the eventual breakup, there were various and sundry efforts aimed at making a difference. Several of them appeared to be brilliant appendages to a major up and coming communications company. The third station owned by NBN was located in New York City. Under the direct supervision of yours truly, it too was a success story.

But somewhere during the earlier years, when Eugene Jackson asked me what I thought of a black news wire service, I mumbled something incoherently as I tried anxiously to overcome the surprise of his assertive attitude about the subject. Then finally, I recovered sufficiently enough to be honest and admit that I had not thought of it at all.

While he continued extolling the virtues of such an innovation on our part and explaining the business model as a coup, one that would yield for NBN authority as the first to provide a service that all black newspapers, radio stations, magazines et el. could tap into. I thought to myself, "My God! This guy's got me tumbling head over heels, down hill again." It made so much sense.

This was another great idea. Therefore as a matter of respect, I had to come back to the scene and let him know that I thought it was something we should do. Then I questioned whether we had access to the resources for such an undertaking. This time he was gentle in reminding me that it was his job to think of it and my job to see that it is done. That having been settled, we agreed to go to our respective corners and meet on the subject at a later date.

In short order, our discussions on the wire service reconvened mainly through the telephone. The solid consensus was that the upcoming meeting of the National Newspaper Publishing Association (NNPA), the premier group of publishers of black newspapers in the world, was where we had to be with this innovation. The NNPA was under the control of Dr. Carlton Goodlett, a psychiatrist who owned a black newspaper in the

Bay Area of California. Dr. Goodlett was President of the group and was planning a big session in Washington, DC. Gene and I knew we had to be there.

In addition, we thought those in attendance would be glad to have us there with this good news. A major plan designed to make the business of covering news for black constituencies bigger and better. This being the agenda in general, we had to make sure that the logistics of our visit as new members were effective and impressive. Gene asked me to talk to as many people as I had access to in trying to work out the feasibility aspects of the wire service. We pulled out all stops.

Somewhere along the line Gene asked the key question: " Vince, how can we demonstrate our sophistication in the news coverage business? He mused on, can we show them how a story from the NBN wires would differ from the general coverage...the gaps our stories would fill?" Plus the added information we get directly from the continent of Africa." By now, the room is filled with invigorated inspiration! Again, the President has sold us another one of his super charged brainstorms.

We agreed that a mocked wire service would be on exhibition at the NNPA conference. This would do it! This would show the owners of all the Black Newspapers around the nation that they are on the cutting edge of a Black News Boon. With the coming of the NBN wire service they would be able to fill their papers with lots of fresh news right off the ticker tape. So we thought.

After making arrangements for the presidential suite in the headquarters hotel, we spent loads of money renting a ticker-tape machine that would feed a teletype machine which we also leased for the duration of the convention. The ticker-tape machine was a product of the technology available in those days. Once we had it erected in one of the bedrooms in the suite, it was impossible for any normal sized human being to pass through that room.

Several of our news persons at the network contributed to the writing of a news summary that was keyed into the ticker-tape system. The teletype machine was then placed in the parlor of the suite. It spewed out stories all day. Our guests strolled through the suite while we hawked the coming of NBN's innovative wire service.

I don't quite know when Dr. Goodlett heard of our contraption or decided he had had enough and invited Gene and me to breakfast. Dr. Goodlett had come alone. I came with Gene but we had not talked about what could come out of this get-together. We had barely gotten past the sipping of our individual juice selections before "all hell broke loose."

I was soon to learn that Gene had again painted us into a corner of bad politics. Right after the good doctor asked, "what the hell are you guys doing?", Gene went into a litany of justifications for a news wire to serve all of the Black Newspapers in the NNPA. Dr. Goodlett pretended he was listening. But, the deep wrinkles in his brow gave him away. He was simply waiting for an opportune point in the conversation to attack Gene with all "four feet."

When the words did start flowing, he was like a hissing adder; trying to get his point across, emphatically, without raising his voice to the spectacle of those seated nearby. Now Gene is listening but with a smirk on his face. Making powerful people squirm was one of Gene's more cherished past-times.

In so many words, Carlton Goodlett made it crystal clear that whatever he wanted his NNPA membership to know about the newspaper industry, he would be the first to tell them. And that, he considered our wire service display a bold and disrespectful intrusion. Gene attempted to counter with some eclectic superlatives aimed at aggrandizing Dr. Goodlett for a job well done. He continued by urging the Doctor to entertain . . . "concepts to take the Black Newspaper industry to another level." Goodlett's unrestrained retort was . . . "Bull Shit!"

Gene is stunned! There is a long spell of silence, for at least thirty seconds, before Dr. Goodlett launches his tirade, with voice trembling as the height of his passion becomes more obvious, trying to explain in profound sincerity that whatever NNPA is or isn't; he built it from scratch, with his money, his time and his ingenuity. Therefore, if there were to be any kind of commercial boon deriving therefrom, he would be the primary beneficiary and not "Gene Jackson and his gang."

We knew the meeting was nearing its end when Dr. Goodlett started using the "N" word. He said: "If I had known you young niggers would be coming in here with this kind of Bull Shit, your attendance request would have been rejected." Gene is assertive beyond reason sometimes but not disrespectful to pioneers such as Dr. Goodlett. He is also intelligent enough to know when to cease fanning sparks to avoid a big blaze. Therefore, we left the breakfast to prepare for compliance with the Doctor's request that we stop displaying our simulated wire service for the duration of the convention. During our recovery meeting back in New York, Gene took his familiar stance and announced that we would continue pursuing the means by which to establish a black news wire service.

When we finally conceded that we had not won over Doctor Goodlett and his cohorts, we then began to speculate that our base market was the radio station. Not just black radio stations but any and all stations whose management sought to satisfy a cross section of the listening population. We, therefore, thought we could get started by signing up as many of them as possible. Then, we would siphon off the good doctor's members at NNPA, one-by-one. But, as it turned out, the radio station owners didn't buy in either. End of story.

At the White House with President Jimmy Carter, Chief Editor Joe Brown and White House Correspondent Simon Frye conduct an NBN exclusive interview. Brown is seated left and Frye to the right facing Mr. Carter.

16

It is somewhat difficult to place these episodes in a ranking order in terms of their value. But, as the saying goes "all things are relative" and NBN's contribution to bringing about the National Association of Black Journalists is second to none. The owners of NBN really wanted this project to happen. This point is most likely a very hard sell because the network had very little presence with NABJ except for my participation in the early days.

The truth of the matter is, this was one of those occasions when Gene and Syd stood with shoulders together and agreed that I should go all out in my support of the development of NABJ. In addition, they appeared to share the same degree of intense enthusiasm for the association. Their foresight might have been a bit keener on this matter than mine. Nevertheless, I gave all we had and more. There were many hours in hotels around the country steeped in engaging debate over the direction we should take in setting up this direly needed organization.

Recollection assures me that most of us knew very well that it was far beyond time to establish this organization; a national body that would do the bidding for the professional known as the "Black Journalist." Oddly enough, however, we found it difficult to identify a concensus on which to build a mission statement; we came in too many colors, figuratively speaking. But, as other African American professionals in a wide range of eclectic fields were doing throughout the nation . . . it had to be done.

The civil rights years had pushed hundreds of black youngsters into communications and journalism schools throughout the country. Many of them emerged exceptionally prepared. And yet, some were looking for an opportunity to "set the records straight" with their own brand of black advocacy journalism. All of this thrown in with the senior black journalists who had been writing his form of advocacy journalism for decades made for a rather strained mixture.

135

These were the stalwarts known from coast-to-coast. Their bylines appeared in our most revered black-owned newspapers. However, except for a miniscule number, they published once a week. This group, though well known in the industry, had not a clue of the pressures faced daily by their younger colleagues at the large newspapers with a sum total of one to two black reporters. These youthful professionals were gathered to find a way to level the playing field. Some of these pressures were perceived and/or concocted but nonetheless forces with which to reckon.

By now, however, several among the founding group had either been nominated or found worthy of a Pulitzer. It is also safe to assume that many of them had already begun to savor the awesome power and preferential reverence enjoyed by journalists who reside at the top of the heap.

Unfortunately, however, these were the least likely to lend a full effort to a movement such as National Association of Black Journalists.

Nevertheless, here in this mix of well-intended professionals, the concordant on "where we must go" was much easier to reach than the "how we must go." The initial meetings were always scheduled adjacent to other events of mutual interest: The Congressional Black Caucus Weekend, The Urban League annual conference, The NAACP annual meeting, et al. In most cases, this assured us a worthy attendance.

The circumstances forcing us to seek a forum through which to address problems perceived as common, also served as stumbling blocks. Ideally, the profile of a core member would have been the journalist who writes for a major daily. Conversely, quite a few were on the job just a short while and carrying various kinds of baggage: 1) Only Black at a daily newspaper in the deep south 2) Not really getting assignments worthy of his/her skills 3) Disagreement with the editor on what should be covered on behalf of black readers and so on...

A good thing for the incubation stages of NABJ was Paul Brock. Paul single handedly served as a catalytic force to keep us in an organizing frame of mind. He used the media files he had compiled during his earlier years at the Democratic National

Committee. His friendships with Mal Johnson of Cox Broadcasting and Chuck Stone of the Philadelphia Daily News added strength to his efforts.

There was a considerable amount of charitable input by Chuck Stone. I characterize his contributions as charitable because if anybody in the group was working on behalf of the institutional causes...it was Chuck. A true veteran, who knew many sides of the issues. He knew and felt the urgent need of an NABJ but at this point in his splendid career, I don't think it would not have mattered.

Chuck Stone was a columnist for the Philadelphia Daily News. In addition to having worked up through the ranks of black weeklies, Chuck Stone was a published author who had worked abroad and served at home as an aide to our distinguished New York Congressman , Adam Clayton Powell. Chuck rolled up his sleeves and met the challenge in the rollout of NABJ.

A considerable amount of credit should go to several other journalists from Philadelphia including Acel Moore, Reginald Bryant, and Joe Davidson. Choosing names for this occasion is risky. Invariably, some worthy being will be left out. But there were several persons in position to get with Brock and establish the nucleus needed. Among them: Mal Johnson, (Cox Broadcasting) Vernon Jarrett (Chicago Tribune) Sarah Ann Shaw (WBZ-TV Boston) Dexter Eure (Boston Globe).

My choice of names from Philadelphia may seem a bit subjective but these guys demonstrated a high degree of passion for the success of both their local chapter and the national organization as well. So much so, they were always in a fight of some kind, either among themselves or at the national level.

Not all those in attendance were practicing journalists. It was obvious there were others who saw the future more clearly than the journalists. They were writers of other sorts; public relations, speechwriters, lobbyists, public affairs and consumer affairs writers for corporate America. For these, NABJ was a boon, struggling for birth and lingering too long in the delivery room.

The memory is still vivid with the author. A renowned young woman who was then a lobbyist for a major oil company was in attendance at the founding meeting. Her national image had been earned some years earlier when she was a recording artist with a hit tune. When she was told that only working journalists could remain in the room, she immediately became one standing picture of indignation; pleading:

"Do you people know what you're doing? I and others like me, are the last persons you would want to evict from your meeting." She went on, pleading . . . "do you have any idea...can you even imagine what my budget is for this very concept you are contemplating?"

Her words fell on indifferent ears. The founding took place without any writers but those who were working journalists. If my recollections are correct, Paul Brock, one of the front runners in this, and himself not a working journalist, was the only such person allowed to remain.

It was my assignment as director of region # two (New York, New Jersey and Connecticut) to organize the local chapter. This is where Gene and Syd agreed that I should spend the necessary amount of money to see that this does happen.

We provided meeting space for more than two years along with food and refreshments for every meeting. Despite the special efforts of several of the female reporters, we were never able to get New York Association of Black Journalists (NYABJ) up and running. With all the basic resources concentrated in the tri-state area, NYABJ should have been the flag ship chapter for NABJ. In his book "The NABJ Story" Wayne Dawkins reports that there was a leadership clash between Les Payne (New York Newsday) and me. I am sure he wrote it exactly the way it was explained to him but it happened just a bit differently. I stepped down from the presidency because Les refused to participate at the leadership level most of the members expected of him.

My stepping down was to avoid any kind of leadership clash. Time would prove that my analysis and subsequent actions were appropriately beneficial to the organization. The time lapse notwithstanding, Les later became president of the national organization and provided some meaningful leadership for NYABJ as well.

The NYABJ records lay dormant for more than two years after I vacated the office. Finally, Lena Sherrod (Bergen Record) came to my office to collect the files and NYABJ was soon resuscitated. The rest is a bit of delightful history of which the founders of NBN are most proud. NYABJ, along with other NABJ chapters around the country, moved on to become a remarkable and much needed force in our industry.

Wayne Dawkins, the bright young writer who understood more than most the significance of documenting the progress of NABJ, sculpted an engaging story of struggle and success. On page 181 of his book, he wrote:

"In 1987, Miami was young, restless, bold, explosive, wildly colorful and of course tropical. NABJ held its 12th convention in this rainbow city, home of " black Americans, white Americans and recently arrived Americans," said Mayor Xavier L. Suarez. The Metro area included 800,000 Hispanics, 400,000 African Americans, 250,000 Haitians and 250,000 Jewish Americans. There were many new faces among the 1400 convention goers: young journalists and new members working at their first newspaper or TV station alongside news veterans who came to reacquaint themselves with NABJ after an estrangement.

Mental stimulation, source-building, fellowship and recreation nourished them. They jousted with Chicago Mayor Harold Washington; were scolded, then rallied on by victorious "Daily News Four" plaintiff David Hardy, and inspired by U.S. Appeals Court Judge A. Leon Higginbotham Jr. "This will recharge my batteries for another six months," said a copy editor from an Ohio newspaper.

DeWayne Wickham, Gannett News Service columnist and owner of Vanita Productions, was elected President, besting Robert Tutman, a network TV photojournalist. Wickham rebounded from a humiliating defeat in 1985. Outgoing President Albert E. Fitzpatrick pointed to a fast-growing association that in two years had:

- Opened a national office in Reston, Va.
- Added a dozen affiliate chapters.
- Increased its treasury by 150 percent, to $500,000 from $200,000.
- Raised $100,000 for a scholarship endowment fund."

Dawkins' book is entitled: "Black Journalists: THE NABJ STORY." It's loaded with the prodigy of American Journalists of African descent. But even he will have to step up the pace to keep abreast of his highly talented and enterprising colleagues. Moving forward to year 2000, NABJ officials reported at their 25th anniversary meeting: 3,000 members, 125 chapters and an annual budget of $2.2 million. This is a very long way from the days when those of us who could, dug deep into our pockets and charged it back to our limited expense accounts to keep the organization afloat.

17

In the sixties, during the heat of the civil rights movement, the awesome power of the news media loomed over the United States from shore-to-shore. With the nation's infrastructure tossed-and-turned by the travails of riots in the cities and racial murders in the rural areas, this country's news media were more racially sensitive than anytime before.

Some white reporters who failed to understand the reason why remedial efforts such as recruitment and accelerated training were necessary to place black reporters in newsrooms around the nation, would surprisingly acknowledge without the least bit of reluctance, that their patriotic mission was to report racial injustice with utter zeal.

Therefore, on the few occasions when such injustices were not boldly parading up and down the streets of our cities, these journalists would form investigative teams to uncover racial injustice. And, chase it right onto some courses of concession and/or correction; and sometimes to the level of prosecution when possible.

By the same token, civil rights leaders themselves had begun to take advantage of this incongruent sentiment. The effectiveness of their campaigns depended on the amount of media on the scene as witnesses and messengers. It then became strategically beneficial to plan activities of civil disobedience with a media schedule in mind. Many courses of action were charted to the convenience of the media.

But, when Reverend Jesse Jackson asked for a slot on the network featuring him as a commentator, I was at a loss for the appropriate answer. If his publicly known credentials were the only consideration, this would have been a no-brainer. Telling him no was a tough job for yours truly.

For starters, I had watched Jesse Jackson as he grew in stature from a local adolescent activist, bent on fulfilling the embodiment of a famed spiritual leader, a world-class orator plus a connected politician. But I was convinced that the skills he used to play the media would later become his major distraction. He is, as of this writing, a TV talk show host, a connected politician who has made two runs at the US presidency.

This highly competitive information/communication society in which we live today places specific demands on those who choose to play. A spiritual leader with news coverage and high level political connections hanging from either shoulder, more than likely will find his spiritual reasoning somewhat "tainted" by his commitment to political and capital gains. But then, according the Shakespeare: "There's nothing good or bad, but thinking makes it so." Or something like that.

These and other considerations flooded my head one day as I watched Jesse Jackson's TV show, "Both Sides." The discussion involved the rapidly growing political strength of Hispanic voters. After the Hispanic spokesman had laid out a list of preferences for presidential candidates Al Gore and George W. Bush. Jesse found the freedom within himself to reduce this moment of sincerity with a "tongue-n-cheek" comment: "They speak Spanish…what do you want?" I blurted: "No…he didn't say that!" Unfortunately, he had.

It had been only a short while since such a statement, reducing the demands of African Americans to such a level of triviality, would have resounded negatively around the world. And I am sure Jesse would have carefully steered away from such public comments, even in jest. But then, the freedom needed to play the role of a modern-day journalist-commentator induces one to add a bit of amusement to the news story.

And we also recall Jesse Jackson as the same personality who " shot himself in the foot" as a presidential candidate with his "infamous" comment about Jews in New York City. Therefore, we now know that our gifted prince is very capable of mixing his disciplines and sounding like a politician when he is supposed to be sounding like a preacher and vice versa.

Some will probably argue that if he is so gifted why not serve both needs, I disagree. Call me a narrow minded purist if you like, but I saw Jesse at his celestial best in 1984 when he went before the nation at the Democratic National Convention. He apologized for the inappropriate remarks about jews and begged his would be constituency to: "charge it to my head and not to my heart." He continued by declaring: "God is not through with me yet." But for all practical purposes, the irreparable damage had been done and he could not get the democratic nomination for president.

But "the measure of the man" was in that same electrifying speech in which he called repeatedly for moral leadership from the White House. He was at his inspirational best that night in San Francisco in 1984. Only one other time did I see him reach so high. It was a decade earlier when the media had contrived a split between him and Reverend Ralph Abernathy over operational procedures at "Operation Breadbasket." Jesse implored Abernathy to back away from reporters goading each of them into a mudslinging, name-calling black leadership spectacle. He publicly declared his affection for Abernathy and credited him with teaching him much of what he understood about the mission.

It was well before the 1984 convention when Jesse called my apartment at about fifteen minutes to midnight. It was a delightful call for my wife, Joyce. Naturally she was thrilled and who wouldn't be. Reverend Jesse Jackson had presided over our wedding ceremonies in Chicago in 1981. There was a sound of restrained glee in her voice as they exchanged a few words of small talk. When she turned to hand me the phone, there was this big question mark of an expression on her face. I gestured: "I don't know why he is calling . . . and particularly at this hour?"

Jesse and I had known each other for a very long time. But, this was not a common occurrence. I was there when he first shared a podium with Dr. Martin Luther King, Jr. in Chicago. Jesse, Dick Gregory and others were leading members of a group called the Coordinating Committee for Community Organizations (CCCO). They were instrumental in Martin's decision to bring his Freedom Festival to Chicago.

Even then, barely over twenty years old, Jesse was the epitome of an aggressive personality. As introductory speaker, his speech was 45 minutes in duration, obviously to the chagrin of his young colleagues. We all stood in the hot sun through the

143

young firebrand's penetrating presentation waiting anxiously to eventually hear Dr. King's first Chicago message.

A bit of related humor comes to mind: while Jesse celebrated the success of his speech. He stepped to the edge of the stage in an utter state of jubilation and yelled an affectionate "hello baby!" Just then one of his teenaged admirers, looking up while she stood near the stage, upbraided him: "Boy! You ain't no preacher . . . calling some girl baby!" In the same idiom, Jesse retorted: "Girl, I'm talking to my Grand-Mama, you be cool!" From my position in the crush of the crowd, I could not attest one way or the other.

Back to my Sunnyside, New York apartment and the near midnight phone call. Jesse's small talk prelude with me was far shorter than the one he had conducted with Joyce. He got right to the core of his keynote question and caught me way off guard: "Brother Vince, who makes the programming decisions at National Black Network?" Quickly, I thought: "Is this a trick question or what? Certainly, he must know that I am in charge of broadcast operations for the network."

I knew I had to eventually answer the question. But, while under the pressure of this realization. . . I also remembered that Jesse Jackson and Gene Jackson were on speaking terms, last I heard. I had remembered a recent occasion when Jesse was exclaiming about Gene having invited him to play basketball on the private court in the back yard at Gene's mansion in Miami but "Gene didn't have no game."

"So, what in the world does he want from me?" I fudged on the answer. " well I guess that's my area of responsibility."

He ignored the implications of that half-hearted reply and began explaining, in a tone somewhat softer than was usual between Jesse and me, that he wanted to do editorials for the network. At first, I did not voice my general opposition to "news makers reporting news" and asked about his vision of the content for these editorials. He explained that they would be about whatever is going on wherever he might be that day or that week. The next thought in my mind: " Right! No plan and my entire staff will be at your beck and call."

I explained that such a practice would take subject matter oversight out of the news room; a condition to which we were not accustomed. He continued plugging away at establishing the essential appeal of a "Jesse Jackson" editorial. But, he fell woefully short on the essential mechanics for operating a news room. The conversation persisted for about three-quarters of an hour with me finally promising that I would bring the proposal to Gene and Syd and thereby have an answer for him by the end of the week. This didn't happen and couldn't have happened. His name had been stricken from a prior list when we considered high profile celebrities having a continued pre-arranged presence on the network; too controversial, too busy, etc.

The death knell for Jesse's proposal came when he requested an NBN reporter be assigned to follow him around the country, and sometimes beyond, just to write the editorials. Secondly, he was not willing to use some of the "Ole' Jesse Jackson clout and charm" to get sponsors for the editorials. It was at this point that I began to feel very uncomfortable about this conversation and started searching for a respectful way to end it.

From a personal point of view, there were several reasons why Reverend Jackson should have had a program on NBN. The first being : There was a very slight chance, if any at all, that his presence would not have attracted the kind of audience numbers needed to sustain the project.

Secondly, I am sure the sponsorship matter could have been arranged with a good deal of specified marketing. In no way, however, would this have precluded a need for Jesse to get involved in the advertising and/or fund-raising end of the project.

A third consideration here would be that we were "home boys" so to speak. During his development days in Chicago, I was a struggling actor and radio personality involved in many of his very intuitive social-change campaigns. In fact, I was indebted to the "Country Preacher!" He and his staff at Operation PUSH spared no amenities during my wedding ceremonies there in 1981.

Aside from all of the real reasons why I could not accommodate Reverend Jackson, there was my conviction that persons spiritually endowed such as he, should be able orchestrate the dynamics of their mission without total reliance on the media; and thereby escape the inevitable vanity that tends to taint and corrupt.

Needless to say, Jesse's work speaks for itself. He has adroitly made use of the media down through the years. And more than likely, could not have pulled off his unique acts of international goodwill except that they be full blown by the media as he planned them. Conversely, I must admit, as Jesse grew in stature during my years as a working reporter, he never turned me down when I needed him for a story. During my final months at NBC in Chicago, he arose from his sick bed to come the studio for an hour long interview. Thanks for everything Jesse!

There was also a surprise when Dr. Benjamin Hooks asked for a commentary spot on NBN. His request came differently. We were sitting in my car at a stop light on 55th street a few blocks from the NBN headquarters in New York City's midtown. Setting up the element of surprise was the fact that there had been no prior discussion of such an undertaking. And he, while reading a newspaper as I drove, suddenly lifted his head and said:

"Why don't you and Gene Jackson let me do some editorials on the network?" Following a pause during which he chose to look up at me from his newspaper...he continued, "you know, you could get Jesse Jackson to do some also. This way we could keep the issues before the black population."

I asked for time to consider this "marvelous" idea. Ben Hooks is also a preacher who was then pastor of two churches, one in Detroit, Michigan and one in Memphis, Tennessee. This was in addition to his full time job as Executive Director of the NAACP. Moreover, he had come to the NAACP fresh from a two year stint as the first African American to sit on the Federal Communications Commission.

The one thing that concerned me most about Dr. Hooks is that he never seemed to consult his watch or a clock on the wall to see if he was making his schedule. And his staff persons never made any attempts to goad him along. His disarming personality

146

would repel all such attempts and he would, in spite of all, routinely show up one to two hours late for the appointment.

And, nobody in his party would have an explanation. I would find myself on the verge of an emotional demand for some form of explanation or apology. It was not to be. Ben Hooks charmed everybody within ten feet of his office and some of those he chose to talk to on the phone.

This day on which he proposed doing a commentary for the network was typical and vividly corroborated my need for concern. It was one of those occasions when he had chosen to come to the phone and the arrangements for his appearance on one of the network's shows. He came to the phone and said: "Brother Saunders...(he always converted my name from Sanders to Saunders) I can do the taping at one o'clock, will that work with your schedule?"

After agreeing to that time slot and a split second before hanging up the phone he yells: "Oh yeah! Brother Saunders would you send a car for me?

"Yes Doc, I'll pick you up personally"

"Good, he said, why don't you get here about eleven thirty. If I get a chance to do it earlier I can just run down stairs to your car."

All of these new arrangements were made without any mentioning of the taping having already been set for eleven thirty, weeks ago, by members of his and my staff.

I arrived on time from my office which was only blocks away. At one o'clock he had not come down. Various members of his staff came to comfort me and assure me that he was aware of my presence. The taping eventually took place at four thirty in the afternoon. But, this was typically Ben Hooks, Executive Director of the National Association for the Advancement of Colored People (NAACP) and other extraordinary achievements.

His scholarship had afforded him, among other things, a law degree. By the time he came to prominence as the first black to sit on the Federal Communications Commission (FCC), he had already been a judge. And while at the NAACP, he was pastor of two churches.

And, if you thought Andy Young was homespun, you needed only to meet Ben and his lovely wife Frances. Not a pretentious notion to be found anywhere near them. They too had been awarded, through his position at the NAACP, an apartment in the high-rent district of New York City. Like The Youngs, Frances and Ben acknowledged that their quarters came with the positions but were not necessarily a prerequisite. The Hooks were perched over the rather exclusive strip known as Central Park South; by all measures, a choice piece of New York City real estate.

His career move from the FCC to the NAACP caught many by surprise. Some of the African American Entrepreneurs in the broadcast industry thought Ben Hooks had jumped ship when there was still so much to be corrected at that level. The transition would prove to be one of major concern at some levels.

His arrival at the NAACP to replace the venerable, Roy Wilkins, was stormy to say the least. Mr. Hooks was greeted with a vigorous power struggle. According to several press accounts, Margaret Bush Wilson and Ben Hooks were finding it very difficult to work with each other. She as chairperson of the national board of directors and he as executive director of the national organization were consistently countermanding each other.

The Reverend Jesse Jackson, Author Vince Sanders and Comedian Tom Dreesen on the occasion of Sanders' wedding to the former Joyce D. Anderson of Chicago. Jackson officiated the ceremony and Dreesen was Sanders' best man.

18

Not all of the African-American movers and shakers bothered to acknowledge the unique mission of NBN. It was a sort of personal sore spot with the author that Charles Diggs, senior member of congress from Michigan, never granted the network not even a twenty-second sound bite.

Then there was the revered Barbara Jordan, from Texas; likewise, she never returned a call from the NBN newsroom. There were probably others that the staff never bothered to bring to my attention. But, those two left me wondering if there was something I didn't understand or something they didn't understand.

The Jimmy Carter White House was acutely attuned to the National Black Network. And, it goes without saying, Andy Young, one of the president's brightest stars, was devoutly in touch with the principles that defined the correlative roles of Black media and Black leaders. And, history will be at a lost to accurately record Andy Young's manipulation of the media in general.

As US Ambassador to the United Nations, he knew that his personal mission aimed at leveling the international playing field, was dangerously unpopular. As some will remember, it was over zealous media that hounded him out of office after he persisted on trying to bring third world nations to the table. On many occasions, he offered information to NBN that the other networks would not touch. After it was fairly certain that Andy would not keep his job of distinction (first African American to serve as US Ambassador to the UN), he prepared himself to leave with a swagger instead of a head hung low.

There were those times when only Black reporters crowded the room high above New York City in the Waldorf Astoria Towers where he reluctantly set up lodging. He often intimated that the towers came with the job but he preferred a little less ostentatious housing. During those sessions, Andy passionately petitioned us not to be concerned. Intuitively, he pointed out, albeit designed to destroy him . . . the media exposure flashing his face all over the world nearly every day was worth millions of dollars in his future. With his new enlarged image, Andy Young, as he promised he would, returned to Atlanta to make it one of the major commercial hubs of the world.

In keeping with the tradition maintained throughout his reign, when it was clear that the other shoe was about to drop, Andy's office called the Black media with individual notification to be there. As fate would paint this bit of history, yours truly just happened to have been standing near the door of the room in which this infamous meeting was being held. When Andy Young emerged, after having been asked to step down from his post, he reached for my hand. His face showed the weariness of a beleaguered warrior. But as we embraced and he pulled away to greet others, he continued declaring himself a winner. The rest is history!

Early on, the Jimmy Carter presidential campaign generated plenty of grist for the National Black Network's mill. There were stories the general media would not cover and in some cases could not fully understand the emotional slant or the cultural depth, thereby underestimating the value of the story. This analysis raises the ire among some who feel that a news story is a news story and it doesn't matter whether it's about African American persons or European American persons. Not true.

For instance, there was a major chasm between black democrats in the Northeast and black democrats in the South. It was all over the enterprising success of Jimmy Carter in attracting the black vote. Many of the main characters in this unfortunate charade will deny any rift existed but it was a natural. It had to happen. The Northeast Cartel which consisted of such seasoned players as Percy Sutton, Borough President of Manhattan, Charles Rangel, Congressman from Harlem, New York, Basil Patterson, New York Secretary of State and Howard Woodson, New Jersey Secretary of State and David Dinkins, who would later become City Clerk and Mayor of New York City, respectively.

This group represented a bastion of political influence before the Carter forces came into focus. The divide began taking shape, however, when the southerners started making noise as if they had the presidency already in the bag. Basil Patterson not only held a power position in his home state that gained him recognition around the country; his appointment to become the democratic party's first black chairman of the National Committee really set him apart. Charles Rangel had been re-elected to remain as the representative from the power-base known as Harlem, and so on.

These stellar public servants had not been accustomed to sharing the political limelight with but a qualified few. They were holding sway in one of the largest urban centers in the nation and thereby influencing large blocks of voters. They had been used to reasoning and working with fellow politicians from Chicago, Detroit, Cleveland and Philadelphia, other large centers of African American voters; but, certainly no farther south than Baltimore and Washington, DC.

One of the most dramatic episodes of this intra-party skirmish came when Jimmy Carter announced his plans to stand on the back of a campaign train and wave to prospective voters from New York City to Chicago. Reporters invited to ride the train were left in the dark on the issue. But it was obvious the Northeast boys had not been asked to join the train as it moved slowly through their territory with an overnight stop in Pittsburgh.

The Carter forces, headed by the less-than-politically-renowned Ben Brown, refused to talk about the situation and Andy Young was nowhere to be found on the train. As the train pulled away from Penn Station in New York City, there were two versions of one rumor abound.

Somebody whispered that Charles Rangel, Basil Patterson and Percy Sutton were on the train but got off in a huff after failing to reach an accord with their fellow democrats from below the Mason-Dixon line. The second version had it: Yes, they did get off because the Candidate, Jimmy Carter, refused to meet with them. However, they would drive on in advance of the train and pick up Howard Woodson and return to the train in Newark, New Jersey.

I spoke to no one who either saw them get on or get off the train at any stop. The white reporters never attempted to report the story. Why? My guess is because they saw no value in it. We also had our limitations with the story. Both sides in the skirmish were careful not to give us too much information on the developments. Nonetheless, it was a good story for the National Black Network. It told about the growing pains borne out of the decade before when we fought for an opportunity to grow.

There were several very telling commentaries buried in this story. The Northeastern contingent of black politicians had not made room for the ultimate surge of their colleagues from the South and the West. On the other hand, it was evident that the Carter contingent had not come to Washington to reason with their Northern colleagues. Many of us speculated as to whether Mr. Carter would have had a longer and less tumultuous stay in the White House if his boys had known more about how to play the game. Of course, that observation was not limited to the black guys on his team. Conversely, Carter's record with the black media was significantly sound. He held several very significant news sessions at the white house arranged especially for the black media.

19

Moving into the second half of the network's inaugural decade was especially exciting. NBN was beginning to get some recognition as a worthwhile purveyor of news and information for and about Black people the world over. On more than a few occasions NBN's coverage included stories from Africa that other news operations either refused or neglected to cover. Our innovative use of the Reuters wire service coverage of East and West Africa gave us a distinctive position in the American news business. NBN introduced this unique Reuters service to the North American region.

Mal Goode, the dean of black reporters, as we lovingly referred to him, was the NBN man at the United Nations. And certainly we were becoming increasingly skillful in ferreting out those stories that most met the essence of our mission on the domestic front as well.

I was rather proud of some of the means by which we got our work done. For a significant span we were directly connected to the sound system in the United Nations' Security Council, enabling us to broadcast, with the simple flick of a switch, any and all portions of speeches by world leaders. Meeting the call of the mission became an easier task as we got to know many of the foreign news-makers and the members of the foreign press as well. And, of course, the National Black Network served as a vital link for African envoys seeking to be heard by the US portion of the Diaspora. It was by no means a small matter in 1976 when the South African Government decided to turnover the first of nine tribal homelands to their respective tribal chiefs. The move was fraught with controversy. Many saw it as a continuation of apartheid. So much so, only one of the other eight Tribal Chiefs came to the Transkei when Kaiser D. Matanzima took over as Prime Minister of the independent Republic of Transkei.

Chief Mangope of Bahputuswana came to the Transkei to cheer on Matanzima in hopes the South African authorities

155

would grant him control of his homeland some time shortly thereafter. The National Black Network enjoyed the privilege and accepted the responsibility of being there in the person of yours truly. Extensive interviews were conducted with both Matanzima and Mangope.

However, I must admit my failures as a professional. My reports, in retrospect, could have been better in terms of intellectual applications. Objectivity was thwarted through failure to keep my emotions in check. Nonetheless, for a chap born on a small farm in Northeast Florida to find himself 41 years later, in a far away land where whites also would rather fight than acknowledge and dignify the humanity in persons with darker colored skin, was uniquely enriching; albeit through the rigid adversity of it all.

The press corps for this event was widely international with a broad range of viewpoints on its value. This was to be expected. In addition, it was fait accompli to find a preponderant number of the white citizens satisfied with the provisions of apartheid. Most of them with which I came in contact held this position while passionately claiming no malice against blacks and coloreds:

"You see Vince, it is far more difficult than you outsiders can understand. It has more to do with politics than the color of a man's skin. We are out numbered in this land and they don't like us. As a matter of fact, some of them don't like each other."

This rationale was readily available whenever a visitor found himself in the unlikely position to listen to it. Being out of position appeared to be easy for me. Therefore, I confronted that bit of preachment more often than I cared to. But in this same context, there were some benefits to be cherished forever. Intermingling with blacks at the hotel I found most to be a gentle people. All were aware of the constant and imminent danger to their personal safety but were not consumed with panic.

However, they did come in varying states of mind. There were those who worked with the system as a means of personal convenience. And there were those who quietly but vengeful recited with resolved conviction "our day will come." In my mind they were both wearing " badges of courage" and living in sanguine faith.

There were several incidents induced by my proclivity to wander off campus at various times when the other media members were under tour guide directions. As I understood it, South African Blacks were not allowed above the second floor of the five star hotel in which we lodged. While in the hotel lobby, getting to know some of the workers, my questions on how to get to Soweto were met with such vague answers as "there is no way to get there" and " I don't think you should go out there, it is not safe." These responses, to say the least, further whetted the appetite. Finally, one of the doormen agreed to arrange the trip through a reluctant cab driver. So reluctant that he charged me fifty rand ($40.US) for a round trip to Soweto.

On our way at a high rate of speed, I made my tape recorder more visible. There is a very quizzical look on his face. I began asking questions to which he gave no answers. To my surprise, my driver either did not or would not speak English. He gestured that I should put away the tape recorder. I asked why. He uttered something, which I interpreted as "no good!" We continued our journey nearing Soweto and I see two very attractive women on the other side of the highway thumbing their way towards Johannesburg. I took note but we kept going.

Upon entering Soweto, I began to realize the fruitless aspect of my trip without a guide who speaks English. So, I asked him to take me to some place where I could maybe talk to somebody. He said emphatically: "no!" To the best of his English-speaking ability he explained that we would be at the peril of the local police; pointing as four of them stood on a corner near their motorcycles. I didn't fully understand but decided to leave matters as they were and asked that we get out of town.

Reenter the two very attractive young women thumbing their way to Johannesburg. As we approached them with their thumbs waving in the air, the driver and I haggled. He conceded at a point in the debate when I couldn't determine if he finally understood what I was asking or did the additional $20 make the difference. He pulls over speaking to them in the native tongue, they asked several questions and peered in through the window

157

at me before finally deciding to both sit crammed into the front seat with him. The taller, lighter complexioned one explained that she was a model and could be seen on the Coke billboards seen along that very road we were traveling. But I could have guessed that. She was a very pretty woman in her early twenties.

They both spoke very good English. And became visibly disturbed by the sight of my tape recorder despite the driver having told them I was a reporter. I lifted the microphone to a level visible from outside the cab and one of them grab the unit and pushed it down and pleaded with me to put it away. The model explained they had no assurances that I was actually who I said I was.

They then reverted to their native tongue and appeared to be chiding the driver for getting them into this predicament. He defended himself and appeared to exonerate me as well. I got that impression when she returned her gaze to my direction as if she was pondering some concern. This lighter moment gave me an opportunity to take the conversation in another direction. I stumbled over every second word trying ask her why was she living in Soweto…a black township. She said proudly I am Zulu, the color of my skin doesn't matter. In this country, it is not your skin color, it is your lineage.

Silently, I scolded myself: "stupid, You knew that…you see a pretty woman and lose control"

Finally and slowly, she is smiling again and explained in a pleading way for me to realize that I could be unwittingly placing their lives in danger. I apologized. She smiled again and immediately began trying to come up with a safe way for me to get an interview. After learning that I was on the fifth floor of the Carlton Hotel, they agreed to come to my room. I expressed my concerns about this kind of arrangement based on the rules I had heard earlier. The ladies convinced me that they could work their way around that obstacle. By this time, my confidence level is very low. When I departed the cab, I was certain that was the last time I would ever see them again.

It was approximately thirty minutes later when the phone rang in my room. The young lady did not give her name. She simply said: "we're coming up." I moved into the hallway to greet them, she waved me back into the room. We entertained a bit of small talk briefly as I began unraveling the cords for the tape recorder. Just then, the telephone rang! It was truly the loudest phone ring I had ever heard. This, of course, was due to the amount of tension in the room at that unsuspecting moment. Almost in absolute unison they each asked: "who is that?"

Simultaneously, I picked up the phone and there was nobody there. They rose to their feet and left the room in a brisk stride...and I never saw them again in life. I was in South Africa for two weeks and never uttered one word about that day to anyone.

The next day as we boarded a luxury passenger train for a trip to the Transkei in time for its independence celebration, I exhaled and felt relieved from the pressures of Johannesburg. We traveled for a full day through some of the most exciting countryside in the world. We gazed at waterfalls that extended seemingly to the sky and animals of all shapes and sizes. While some frolicked through lush green bushes others feasted on bountiful provisions from the natural environs. I am not sure I didn't exclaim loudly while attempting to silently muse: "My God! No wonder so many people want this land. It is the prettiest place on earth."

We entered the press quarters in the Transkei and still vivid in my memory is the first young man I observed upon arrival. His sailor cap was turned upside down as many of the young men wore them in the United States. His mannerisms were no different than any fellow I might have known from Any Neighborhood, USA.

I was delighted when he eventually came over and introduced himself as a photo journalist with one of the local Johannesburg newspapers. Again my emotions started connecting conditions and concepts. He said his name was Ronnie Quai (K-way) and began proudly telling me of the strong sentiment of identification with American Blacks among his peers.

Immediately I could see the emotional similarities to conditions mainly in the southern states at home. This would, more than likely, speak to the differences found among other

African peoples I had observed. Though they too were under oppressive colonial rule, the oppressor had not chosen to live among them and try to maintain a yoke of direct servitude, as had the Afrikaners.

Ronnie introduced me to many of his friends during the Transkei independence inaugural ceremonies. I took particular note of the fact that the festivities were held in a spanking brand new Holiday Inn built especially for this occasion in the Transkei capitol, Umtata. The Singer sang all of the same songs a Jazz singer would sing here in the States. Her name was Sarah. She had worked in London and Paris but not in the United States.

After the show, we left the Holiday Inn and went to the home of a community matriarch known to the entire region as Sister Besse. I had seen Sister Besse many times before but never expected to find her here. Just as I remembered from my youthful days in the Southern United States, Sister Besse was frying fish and chicken, enough for any and every person who came into her small but very neat home. Gradually, I am beginning to get a perspective on the traditions and mores that must have migrated with my fore-parents, willy nilly, from Africa to the shores of the Americas. It was truly an enriching experience.

No doubt some of the persons present caught me staring at them and wondered why I appeared lost in this mesmeric gaze. Example: A very fair skinned, bespectacled man stood in the middle of Sister Besse's living room floor waiting patiently while her out of date stereo system slowly moved from one tune to the other. It was obvious he had been drinking, maybe not too much, but certainly enough to boost his personality. He danced, not very well, to every recording while making jovial conversation with everyone who entered. I was sure I had seen this guy before doing those same uncoordinated steps.

Upon his learning that I was from New York, he immediately began referring to the "Big Apple" and pledging that his next trip will include the "Big Apple." A continuation of his speech revealed that he had barely left the Transkei, let alone the continent of Africa. He danced on and on…alone, to every record. He kept on dancing and dreaming…dancing and dreaming…and dreaming and dreaming. Yeah…I had seen this man many times before in a land far away called the United States. Not only that, he looked in physical appearance very much like those I had seen before. So many similarities.

The following day, we gathered in a large stadium for a continuation of the ceremonies. Before the Political speeches got started there was music and singing performed by some of the world's most beautiful voices. No one in the grandstand, that is no one seated near me, had an explanation as to why one of the tribal dancing groups contained a white female with long straight blond hair. When I continued asking about what appeared to me as an apartheid contradiction, somebody within listening range finally informed me: " Oh she lives up there with them and smiled approvingly." I abandoned the topic and resumed watching the ceremonies.

When the new Prime Minister, Kiaser D. Matanzima, took the podium there was a thunderous outpouring of appreciation. He bade his constituency to turn a deaf ear to doomsayers and understand that Transkei was truly independent and would stand resolved as a non-racial society. The racial issue in South Africa was fraught with intrigue. There was race mixing that appeared unnoticed yet there were many young men and women fearing for their safety from day to day.

20

The network was forging through new frontiers as it headed toward the end of the 1970's. And those of us associated were under watchful eyes from many quarters. This awakening came after a rather puzzling meeting in Boston with Paul Brock who was then working for the Democratic National Committee. We were joined by a radio executive named Paul Yates and Bertram Lee, then a local Boston businessman. I had not met Yates and Lee. My invitation to Boston came from Paul Brock ostensibly on some agenda Basil Patterson was fulfilling as deputy chairman of the Democratic National Committee. It never entered my mind that this meeting was a prelude to some other career move under consideration by my buddy, Paul Brock.

It was Yates who led off. The tenor of his speech characterized Gene Jackson as a misguided bumpkin with not even a clue of how to handle the success of his radio network. Naturally, I was offended but held my peace through surmising, at least for this occasion, that this erudite gentleman is somewhat shy of the facts. And maybe, as the lunch conversation continued I would be able to shed some light on our philosophy at the network. Yates was president of Sheridan Broadcasting, owner of stations in Boston, Massachusetts and Buffalo, New York. Bert Lee, who at the time owned a printing firm, was introduced to me as Paul Yates' business advisor. None of this impressed me one way or the other, unfortunately.

Throughout the lunch, I found myself fielding very probing questions about how and why we did things at the network. Some were forcefully worded and others were rudely intrusive. As it turned out, I sat there like the bumpkin Yates had depicted as an image for Gene, and tried to maintain a genteel demeanor. I never for a moment realized that, Paul Brock, had set me up. I never took time to evaluate the entire picture. I was the only experienced broadcaster at the table and I had not a clue as to the aspirations of these other persons. Paul Yates was already in the radio game and apparently came along to keep the discovery mission on track.

I don't know if the results for them were worth the effort but I do know that Bert Lee went on to become a very viable and rich broadcast owner. Some months later, the two Pauls summoned me to a hotel room in Washington, DC. Yates' group had purchased interest in the Mutual Black Network and hired Paul Brock to be my counterpart. Brock evidently convinced Paul Yates to hire me to fill the obvious experience gap and at the same time eliminate me as a competitive factor.

I eventually caught on and concluded that there was no other reason they would have paid for my flight ticket and hotel room. These talks were as reasonable as they could be, given my new slant on Paul Brock's intentions. For some inexplicable reason, I got the impression they did not believe me when I told them their offer was nowhere near my deal at NBN. Yates said in a gruff tone:

"If your loyalty prevents you from moving up the career ladder, so be it."

After becoming apparently irritated, Paul Brock blurted: "Well, Vince, you don't expect me to pay you, as my assistant, more than I'm making, do you?" My response was enough to make even my daddy proud. I said rapidly: 'yes! if I am worth more to the company than you are." Yates was more than visibly amused at my boastful retort and the meeting ended.

The Mutual Black Network later became the Sheridan Black Network with Paul Brock in charge of news operations. That arrangement lasted about a half year. Various reasons were offered for Paul's early split with Sheridan, depending on who tells the story. Later, Paul did mention that his long time pal and former New York Secretary of State, Basil Patterson, was handling his legal action against Sheridan.

Shortly afterwards, Paul came to New York City as the Press Relations executive for Dr. Benjamin Hooks at the NAACP. And, guess what! Yep, we became buddies again. However, this time when he set me up, it was to my advantage. He introduced me to my second wife, the lovely Joyce Anderson.

A couple of years later when Joyce and I announced our wedding plans, we were offered the greatest compliments possible from two men I hold in the highest of esteem. Dr. Hooks, gleefully offered to perform the ceremonies. It was at that point that I had the socially uncomfortable task of informing him that plans had been made in Chicago, with Reverend Jesse Jackson officiating. He shook his head in approval and my hand in a congratulatory manner. It is worth noting here that Joyce was on Dr. Hook's press relations team, answering to Paul Brock.

A similar occurrence involved former New York City Mayor, David Dinkins. David had not yet made his trek to the front office of City Hall. He was then serving as New York City Clerk. During a casual chat, Mr. Dinkins reminded me that his lovely wife was named Joyce also. He then informed me that part of his responsibilities as City Clerk was the issuance of marriage licenses. He said he would be honored to personally stand in the stead of his staff, issue the licenses and perform the ceremony as well. Mr. Dinkins was as gracious as had been Dr. Hooks when I told him that we would be getting married in Chicago by Reverend Jesse Jackson.

Gentlemen, wherever you are! You made Joyce and me feel very special.

21

"Tell Vince Sanders if he wants me to do that show on his network, he'd better meet me at my lawyer's office in Manhattan at 4 o'clock"

That's the way my assistant, Lynn Hamilton quoted Don King. And as she read the disbelief on my face, Hamilton reinforced her message: "Honestly, that's the way he said it, he called about a half hour ago." There was nothing I could say at that moment to let her know that she was not the source of my disbelief. Lots of changes had taken place since I offered Don King a show on the network. So, why all of a sudden he wants to do a show in which he never expressed any interest before. In fact, I was somewhat insincere when I offered the show. "Don King, please... this is Vince Sanders, returning his call." On the other end, a female voice answered for Don King. It was Celia Tuckman, Executive Director of Don King Productions. "Hi Vince...Don King wants to talk to you about doing that show on the network. "Oh yeah!" But I'm thinking "yeah right!"

"He wants you to meet him at his lawyer's office on the Eastside at 4 o'clock." She continued rattling off the address..."can you be there on time?"

"Yeah...you know what exactly he wants to talk about?"

"He needs to go over the plans for the show."

I hurried to hang up the phone so I could figure out what is going on with Don King? It was the early spring of 1990 when I offered him a slot on the network. The year was moving away fast. I had all but forgotten that I had made the proposal.

These were not the best of times for Don King and his image. Mike Tyson had lost his heavyweight Title and Don came in for some stiff criticism from the press. Many of the sports writers accused Don of being insensitive to the socialization needs of his young fighter who was continually facing scrapes with the law.

It became public knowledge that Mike Tyson was beginning to see Don King in a different light. Tyson began seeking relief through a closer relationship with some of his street buddies thereby shutting Don King out of his affairs.

In addition...there was Bill Cayton, the man who had been handling Tyson's management matters before Mike became entangled with Don King. Cayton was business partner to Cus D'Mato....the renowned boxing trainer who discovered Tyson. All the media attention to the faltering relationship of Mike Tyson and Don King prompted Cayton to make an attempt to rescue Tyson from King. This exploded into a big high profile court battle.

Don King and I had already had our little separation chat after I failed to show up in Japan to broadcast the Tyson/Douglas fight. Through all of this, Tyson was still the best known name on any boxing marquis. The mere mention of his going into the ring would escalate into a discussion of millions of dollars. Cayton knew this. And well did he know that Don would not step aside and allow him to have control of the world's best known heavyweight boxer.

As these two titans prepared to do battle in the courts, the media reports all but predicted that Cayton would emerge the victor. Watching these developments with more than a casual interest, I was seduced by the media's "fool's gold" and began allowing some distance between Don King and me and wooing Bill Cayton for the audio rights to Tyson's upcoming fights.

My first attempt to build a relationship with Cayton was the ultimate in lame gestures. When I first thought of it, a team of wild horses couldn't have prevented me from giving it a try. However, the big bowl of gorgeous looking fruit my assistant was asked to have delivered to Cayton's hospital room was flat out rejected by Mr. Cayton himself.

During the heat of preparation for his slugfest with Don King in the courtroom, Cayton was hospitalized. Every move he or Don made in those days was in the newspapers. Cayton's hospitalization was no exception.

I am still convinced that it was a good first move. My assistant, instead of sending the fruit to the hospital and letting the little candy stripes figure out to which room this man of wide ranging celebrity was assigned, she called Mr. Cayton himself and asked him for his room number. Naturally, his response was:

"who wants to know?"

" Mr. Vince Sanders"

"Who is he?"

"Oh, I am sorry, I thought the two of you knew each other….Mr. Sanders is Vice President of NBN Sports, Inc. ….he wants to send you a basket of fruit."

"For what…..keep it, I don't want any fruit!"

"Yes sir."

At this point, a slight setback was conceded with a dogged resolve to get back to Mr. Cayton at a more opportune time. Meanwhile, let's go back and review some of the early aspects of the rift between Don King and Mike Tyson.

So, one afternoon prior to the evolving of the above mentioned events, I was driving along on the Grand Central Parkway headed toward the Long Island, New York area trying to prepare myself mentally as I do before teeing off at the golf course. Suddenly the mobile phone rang. The voice on the other end said:

"Vince, this is Don King."

Following a long pause while I tried to figure out the reason for this unusual call and prepare myself for it, I responded: "Hi Don." And just then, that familiar sound of static heard when a cell phone is on the verge of cutting out, replaced Don's voice. Instantaneously, the phone is dead, giving me the much needed minutes to figure out how did he get the mobile phone number. Almost immediately, I concluded that my assistant, Lynn Hamilton, decided it would be OK to give my mobile number to Don King. Don King Productions and NBN Sports had already partnered on a couple large events.

While trying to re-dial Don's office, I drove along one of the nation's fastest parkways, still strapped for an answer to the question of ..What's on Don King 's mind?

The call to Don was already connecting and he was on the phone post haste. His first utterance was: "Is this your car phone number?"

"Yeah!...how are you? "

This phone call was not a common occurrence. I had known Don King since 1974 when he promoted the Ali/Foreman spectacular in Kinshasa, Zaire. Over the years, I had attended many of his extravagant parties designed to impress the media. However, I could never find a comfort zone in one-on-one conversation with Don. It was always difficult to determine if in fact he was listening to me.

He appeared otherwise occupied with his eyes darting throughout the room and laughing when nothing funny has been said.

There was one exception, however, that held a lasting spot in my memory. It was in the courtyard at the rear of Caesar's Palace in Las Vegas. In the early days of King's campaign to convince the gaming moguls that casinos and boxing events shared the same market segment, he staged several major boxing matches in the courtyards at the rear of Caesar's Palace.

On this occasion, Muhammed Ali was there to do battle with Ron Lyle...and in his usual style he had ridiculed his opponent by calling him " Mr. Acorn-Head." Lyle wore a cleanly shaved head long before Michael Jordan made it popular on the basketball court.

This was the afternoon before the event, May 15, 1975 when the press representatives from Don's office and those from the casino would register the reporters covering the boxing match. Don and I were leaving the courtyard at the same time, headed toward the casino. Our chat started out with my responding to his query on NBN's success. Media was always a good topic for Don. I diverted the subject to thank him for having introduced me to former heavyweight champion Joe Louis in the Casino lobby the evening before. In his waning years, Joe was hired as host in the lobby at Caesar's.

Before I could get the words out, Don was pulling away from me with a trailing comment..."This woman over here wants my autograph!" The lady was standing deep in about thirty rows of chairs with full vision of her face obliterated by a camera as she continued snapping photos. It was a mind boggling mystery to me how he concluded at that distance that this was one of his fans. As he approached the lady, she looked at him as if she thought he was a panhandler and began rapidly pulling back from him. To prevent any further embarrassment, I turned my back and was looking away when he peered in my direction.

I hasten to say this incident occurred in the mid 1970's, and I seriously doubt that it could have happened anytime thereafter, even if she were a foreign visitor as I had concluded then. The moral of my story is it seemed I never had the right stuff to capture even a small degree of Don King's attention. And it also seemed that anything and anybody who had the potential to pay homage to Don could get his attention fairly easy.

So years later, when he stood still long enough for me to talk him into allowing NBN to have the audio rights to some of the most exciting boxing events of the century, I felt as if I had scored the once in a life time deal. Yet as fate would apparently have it, twenty years later, I find myself still significantly on the periphery of the Don King legacy, which undoubtedly will go down in American History as one of the world's greatest spectacles.

And it picks up again where he is calling me in the car; the cell connection is much better: "I expected to see you in Japan" His reference was to the upset of the century, Buster Douglas' expertly crafted knockout of King's premier boxer, Mike Tyson. Not really prepared for this discussion, I mumbled something about the absence of a signed contract.

This time his voice registered a more emphatic tone, "Vince, why weren't you in Japan for the fight?"

" Don, I didn't have a contract!" I retorted as sternly as I thought I could without exacerbating the situation. Then reminded him: "I signed the contract six weeks before the event and your office never sent it back with your signature."

"What do you mean? you knew we had a deal."

"Are you kidding? You didn't expect me to carry a broadcast crew all the way to Japan without something in writing that says we had the broadcast rights to the fight...did you?"

The Don King public image had broadened dramatically since we met in 1974. It was now widely known, Mr. King was an ex-con who overcame two charges of murder to emerge as

171

one the smartest deal-makers in the world. He had been described as having an uncanny penchant for mathematics and a desire to know every word in the dictionary. The general perception is that this self-styled education aided King in his quest to become a ruthless opportunist, one who left piles of carnage in his path to international notoriety and immeasurable wealth.

This is the likeness Syd and I faced when we decided that we would seriously seek the audio rights to his fights. During our early deliberations on the project we rationalized, using some sparse bits of research to support our initial notion. It was simply this: There must be millions of people who are available to, and indeed would listen to a championship boxing match on the radio. They had done it in years gone by, why not now.

At the peak of Mike Tyson's reign as heavyweight champion of the world, Don King agreed to grant me the radio rights to all of his fights. This was more or less a handshake agreement, allowing Don the freedom of doling out individual agreements to his convenience. Syd was very uncomfortable with this arrangement. So was I. But I knew full well that it was this or nothing at all.

Before the scheduling of the Buster Douglas match in Japan, we had already broadcast three of Tyson's fights with a considerable amount of success. In addition to realizing that there was money to be made through advertising sales, there was a secondary market for the audio rights as well. During the first two matches...Tyson/Holmes and Tyson/Williams...officials at NBN and Don King Productions began to acknowledge the vitality in bringing big time boxing back to radio.

Armed Forces Radio called for permission to pick up our signal. It was agreed Don King Productions and NBN would provide the radio broadcasts of the fights free of charge for the troops serving abroad. Had we gone through with the Tyson/Douglas deal, there was an agreement for subletting of radio rights to large sports coverage firms operating in two foreign countries.

However, three weeks before the match in Japan, Don King's administrative person, Ms. Celia Tuckman, had failed to return the contract with the usual Don King signature. Following several phone calls and no contract, Syd and I made an executive decision. We had no contract therefore we had no deal with Mr. King. Frankly, we had garnered only a third of the sponsorship money needed to break even. It was, to some degree, a catch-22 affair. Because we had no contract, we were reluctant to push our sales staff into promising something we didn't in fact have. This was basically a first. Tuckman and King took their own sweet time delivering previous agreements but never had they failed to send one at all.

Again back to that call to my mobile phone. The small talk lasted far longer than I had anticipated. Nonetheless, I was fully aware that any minute now I've got to come clean and confess to the great Don King that I had in effect thrown down the gauntlet, challenging his customary way of doing business...or not doing business! For some strange reason, it never got to that point. When I emphatically reiterated my concern over the lack of a signed contract...there was a lull in the conversation.

When he did restart the chat he murmured: "Well , she won't do it again...I bet she won't do it again! Now, the ball is back in my court but I am not sure about how I should decipher that last proclamation.

Was he going to punish Celia Tuckman for not delivering the contract? No...I don't think so! But, it certainly sounded that way. But I knew it couldn't be that way because there was no way anything could go on in Don King's office that he didn't know about. In fact, I remained convinced that it was he who withheld the contract. "Nooo...I don't think so!"

When the reality check hit home, I knew precisely what he was saying; "no more deals for you Vince Sanders!"

This was a common practice with Don. He would consistently remind everybody involved that we were all playing with his bat and ball. In addition, we were playing on his ball field and he could take his bat and ball and chase everybody off the field at a moments notice. However, it was my mission to remain calm and collected during this phone conversation. So, I didn't respond one way or the other.

This was not startling news to Syd and me. We had reasoned between ourselves that our absence in Japan would probably end the relationship. To this point we had broadcast only three fights. These were enough to get a feel for the potential. We suspected that Don King had begun to assess the money-making possibilities as well. When I told him about the shortfall of advertising for the Japan fight, he continued:

"Let me tell you guys something, I get my money! I get my money! I don't be bullshitting about my money!"

Again, I am confronted with a double entendre: " Is he advising us on how to get money from advertisers or is he threatening me again?" Remembering that the better part of valor is discretion. I chose to "keep cool"...I did just that. Not once during the conversation did I ask a question or offer a comment that would further heighten the tension. It didn't really matter. I had concluded the arrangement was on its final leg.

All of these machinations were in line with Don's gradual recognition that there was at least an additional dollar to be made through championship fights on radio. Certainly, radio revenues were far from those available for television boxing matches. But, there were some decent bucks to be made. Another stumbling block was the several occasions when we found advertisers refusing to get involved with a Don King fight.

In our initial search for a blow-by-blow announcer we found a lad who was an ABC television sportscaster in Chicago. We flew him into Atlantic City to do the blow-by-blow on Tyson/Holmes after our Sports Director, Ron Pinkney performed the task for the rollout bout featuring Mike Tyson and Carl Williams. During the first production, former heavyweight Champion, James "Bonecrusher" Smith did the color commentary. Many fight fans of that era will remember all the hype about Bonecrusher being the first boxing champion in the country with a college degree. The color for the second bout was handled by then leading heavyweight contender, Evander Holyfield.

We were headed for tall cotton by the time fight number three came about. Former lightweight boxer Randy Gordon who was serving as Athletic Commissioner for the State of New York under Governor Mario Cuomo, graciously put aside his governmental status and returned to the ringside for the NBN Sports blow-by-blow of the fight between Mike Tyson and Michael Spinks. Following his boxing career and before his political stint, Randy had been a sports writer with Ring Magazine.

This arrangement would turn out as one of our brighter moments. This one brought home some bacon. Anybody familiar at all with the scene of a boxing match with which Don King is associated, knows clearly who is first in the ring, ostensibly to congratulate the winner. Those of us closer to the scene are acutely aware of the amount of time and energy expended plotting to keep Don King's image before the TV camera. And fortunately for all the stations affiliated with the NBN Sports network for the fight, this event was no exception.

Somewhere in the dynamics of this star-studded evening, where people were so densely mingled that it became a chore to simply stand in one location, Randy Gordon made Don King aware of his presence at ringside and his desire to interview Mike Tyson at the sound of the final bell.

Now I ask you...how powerful is this? State Athletic Commissioner, the man who is charge of regulating professional sporting events throughout the State of New York, asking the nation's premier sporting events promoter for a gesture of cooperation. I apologize for the insinuation and hasten to explain that there is no stigma here. Don King couldn't earn enough money to pay his car service bill with a fight at Madison Square Garden.

For all practical purposes, the Garden was the sum total of Randy's jurisdiction. Championship boxing at Madison Square Garden had been a thing of the past for so long many of us barely remembered. Moreover, with Don King at the helm of professional boxing, and the absence of gambling casinos in Manhattan, professional boxing will never return to the hallowed heyday of Madison Square Garden.

Better than we had envisioned, the moment the referee hoisted Mike Tyson's gloved hand toward the ceiling, Don King was moving from the end of the ring where he had climbed up in a split second, emphatically cupping Tyson's elbow and ushering him through a swarm of reporters and their TV cameras right on through to Randy Gordon...allowing him the first interview immediately after the fight. Need I say, as executive producer, how much pride surged through me. I had reason to think inwardly: " Man, this is going to be winner. It's catching on !"

As I continued pondering NBN Sport's fight project and its awesome potential, my angel messenger on my shoulder kept whispering...urging me to wake up! The odds were stacked against progression. Don had Already begun to ask for too much money up front. Secondly, he was withholding his approval of each deal until within weeks of the actual event. Thirdly, several of the major advertisers who spend considerable sums to reach fight fans admitted they were displeased with Don's business practices and chose not to cooperate with NBN.

So, you might conclude that our decision not to go to Japan was in protest of the negative points just mentioned. And now, I am driving along, talking to Don King and anticipating a throw-down of the gauntlet. But just when I thought the phone call was about to end, he seamlessly moved away from my absence in Japan to the media reports on Mike Tyson's loss to the little-known Buster Douglas.

"Everybody blaming me...the boy didn't fight, shit I wasn't in the ring ... he was in the ring!"

Frankly, I hadn't paid any particular attention to what the sportswriters were saying about one of the most surprising upsets in boxing history. But, I could tell immediately that Don King's ire was up and he would make an effort to set the record straight.

When I started inquiring as to the identity of the sportswriters in question, in his usually cunning manner, he refused to name a single person. Nor did he implicate any of the media organizations. Instead, Mr. King continued attempting to distance himself from the role of a father image for one of the world's most famous orphans.

"I can take him to the ring, that's my job....but he does the fighting, I don't fight, that's Mike Tyson's job. Instead of criticizing me...they should be taking note of how good the promoter does his job"

At this point, I felt the conversation was becoming a bit friendlier and made a fumbling attempt at easing the tension.

"So, what's going to happen to Mike now?"

There was a brief pause indicating that he wanted to be sure of his answer. And, while he prepared to answer, I realized that I had not chosen the most sociable question for the occasion.

" I don't know what's going to happen …I don't know what he's going to do…I'm the fight promoter, not the fighter."

I couldn't remember if I had ever seen Don King in such a remorseful or concerned mood about anything. Apparently, all of the press about King taking advantage of Tyson's youth and lack of sophistication was finally beginning to take it's toll on King. Cus D'mato, the boxing guru who had adopted Tyson from the crime ridden streets of Brooklyn, New York and taken him to a virtually all white middle class environment in upstate New York, had passed on just as Don King was becoming an indelible part of Tyson's boxing career.

There was a considerable amount of media speculation about who would take up where Cus left off. The gossip pages who followed this 20-year-old, super rich famous Black celebrity around demonstrated to us all that there was still plenty to be done in the raising of Mike Tyson. And, as time would eventually reveal, what with Tyson's prison terms and squandering of large sums of money, the job was never completed.

There were those journalists with courage enough to demand that Don King, based on the amount of money reaped from the existence of Mike Tyson, take Tyson under his wings socially. In another camp, we found those who were naive enough to believe that Don would automatically begin caring for Tyson and his millions as did Shelly Finkel for Champion Boxer, Mark Breland. According to press reports, Finkel arranged financial instruments that will deliver Mark from any forms of worry about money the rest of his life. Hats off to you Shelly! Help Mike, if it's not too late.

To my surprise, Don King's call to me on the mobile phone ended without him declaring our relationship down and out for the count. As he hung up, reiterating that he was not responsible for Mike Tyson's loss of his title to Buster Douglas, I was still somewhat unclear about his concerns regarding the media. This certainly wasn't the first time the press had come down hard on Don King. As a matter of fact, Don King always appeared to relish negative press; it provided forum for his verbosity. At any rate, my attention was more toward the loss of the broadcast opportunity than who or what caused Tyson to lose his crown.

Subsequent to the phone call, Syd and I got together in a commiseration session. While acknowledging that without Don King our boxing division of NBN sports was " up the creek," so to speak, we continued trying to conjure a strategy. It was decided that I would approach the other two promoters, Bob Arum and Dan Duva. They both said yes but there were no fights of note on the docket at either location. Arum had Sugar Ray Leonard's much talked-about return from retirement again, but no one was certain of the date and who he would fight. Duva was hanging with Evander Holyfield who had not yet become a marquis attraction.

Arum suggested we broadcast some of his club fights until the big events came to fruition. Couldn't happen! The cost of production for a little card was as expensive as for a big card. Advertisers don't sponsor club fights. Around the same time, there were some questions looming regarding Holyfield's health. There was one thing eventually very clear to Syd and me, if in fact we ever had any options, they are now condensed to one final element and his name is Don King.

Following a suggestion from Syd, I embarked upon a confidence mission. Don's voracious penchant for the media attention was universally known. Since Don will do anything to keep his face before the microphone or TV camera, my task should be easy. I will offer Don King an opportunity to have his own show on the network. He will be awe-struck! But only for a minute or two, just before he replies with a resounding ...yes! This will bring him closer to us and...you get the picture?

Well, when I called Don to suggest the show, He wasn't awe-struck nor did he say ...yes! There is a strong possibility he said softly: " yeah right!" One thing for sure, he never got back to me on the proposal as he said he would, not even after several

178

follow up calls. So, why am I to believe, many months later that Mr. King is truly interested in doing a show on the National Black Network? I don't!

I arrived at this large Eastside office building where I looked up and saw the name of the law firm that had been given to me by Celia Tuckman. The name was on the outside of the building, in human sized lettering, indicating that this law firm either owned this towering building or was the major tenant of this opulent structure. Either way...some heavy duty legal fees are connected here. It was now 10 minutes before 4pm and I have yet to park and get up to the floor of the meeting. I was later than planned because I drove by headquarters office to pick up Syd.

We entered the floor at about 4:05pm...five minutes late. They were standing in the center of the waiting area, four persons including Celia Tuckman but no Don King. Syd and Celia had not met before. I introduced them and she was the ultimate in diplomatic behavior. She did confirm that this group of lawyers owned the whole building, from top to bottom. If Syd was impressed, he didn't show it. He too, as was I, wondering why we needed all of these people to discuss a radio show that isn't going to happen in the first place.

Don King entered with his lawyer from Chicago. Now it's six of them and just Syd and me; two thirds of them are lawyers. It might have been more than that, I seem to recall Celia telling me that she had a law degree. Don's hello was cold and dry. We took seats on the same side of this long expensive looking table. There is a body to my right separating me from Don King and Syd is at my immediate left. Celia and two of the guys took seats facing us with the Chicago guy at the head of the table near Don King. As we settled at the table there were groups of small talk going on while I am trying to force some conversation about the "Don King Radio Show."

Immediately, the barrister from Chicago put a damper on my efforts with his opening statement. Looking directly at me he asks:

"Is this the young man who offered $365,000. for the radio rights to the next Tyson fight?"

179

I can't answer right away...Syd is cautious also. I don't know what motivated Don King, maybe an attempt at levity to take off the edge of the situation. But he was next to speak: "No, Vince Sanders didn't do that. I know Vince better than that...he didn't do that."

The amusing thing to me was that Celia was just about to respond in the affirmative before Don' s assertion interrupted her....she had already said: "Yes, that's......"

I looked at Syd and he was starring at me...simultaneously we shook our heads...indicating that NBN had not offered anybody $365,000. for a Tyson fight. The Chicago guy took the lead again, asking me:

"How much did you offer....Bill Cayton?"

"I didn't offer Mr. Cayton anything for the rights to the fight"

At this point, one of the lawyers seated across the table asked:

"Are you saying you did not make Bill Cayton an offer for the radio rights to any of Mike Tyson's fights?"

" I did not make Bill Cayton an offer for any Tyson fights." I answered.

Since we were seated on the same side of the table with another person in between us, Don and I had to lean considerably forward to make eye contact and he was not trying very hard until this point: "Where did the $365, 000. figure come from?"

"Well, actually I sent Cayton a proposal letter in which I stated that the gross advertising revenue could possibly reach that amount for a Mike Tyson fight on radio."

Meanwhile, Syd was flipping pages in his briefcase. He was thoughtful enough to bring his Don King file folder...I didn't and therefore did not have a copy of the letter. And boy did I need it to avoid overstating its contents. He nudged me signaling that he had located the letter, then handed it to me. I began perusing it....and one of the legal voices seated at the table said: "we would like to have a copy of that letter"

"No!" Syd said in a low voice and my rejection followed his for everybody to hear.

"No we can't let you have this letter!" Syd said.

It was then that Don King "lost it" for a brief spell. He leaned forward in his seat and yelled: "Then I'll subpoena your ass!…Son-Of-A-Bitch!"

One of his legal minions seated on the other side of the table shushed him down and he returned to his "only in America" smile.

I was amused…I had never seen Don in that state of mind. But now, we are at an impasse. While some peripheral comments were bandied about, I noticed one of the legal men had left the table. Syd offered a suggestion: "We are not going to release this letter but we will give you a letter detailing our proposal to Bill Cayton"

Somebody at the table said "we'll take it." Suddenly, the gentleman who had been sitting across from me is back and sliding a piece of paper in front of me. It's an affidavit containing verbatim snippets of my comments at the table. While shoving the paper at me, he is taking the cover from a pen and handing it to me. A quick glance revealed what I needed for my decision. While handing it on to Syd, my reply was emphatic: "No….I can't sign that"

Syd was a resounding echo: "we're not going to sign that!"

An exasperated voice somewhere in the room blurted: "send us the letter!"

The fellow with the unauthorized affidavit took his handy work back into a nearby room and others in the group were busy containing the big man…Don King.

With this, Syd and I began facing reality. The big meeting about a Don King Show on NBN, the meeting with four, maybe five lawyers, was coming to an end; coming to an end without even a sincere mentioning of the Don King Show. This is where NBN's foray into the fight game also met its eventual end.

We sent the letter to Don King's lawyers and history continued writing itself with "guess who" emerging as winner over Bill Cayton. This meant that Don King was still the undisputed promoter of heavyweight championship boxing, " in the world!."

There is a big chance this book would not have been written had matters resulted differently. Shortly after our fight projects fell through, the network began to falter financially. A success with the fights could have prevented its folding by yielding a cushion of cash. So, the network Roy Wood brought into my experience was declared deceased toward the end of 1990.

It was through this period when I remembered Don King casually mentioning something about starting a radio network and broadcasting his own fights. You would think I had enough by now. But I thought: "what the heck, perchance he really wanted to do this." So I sent him a letter offering my services in setting up his network. He never answered. When we did eventually meet again, we grinned at each other as though nothing had ever come between us. I think we might have even taken another picture together.

Meanwhile, Syd was sending signals that he did not want to renew my agreement with the company, thereby bringing an end to a very successful run we had enjoyed at WWRL radio in New York City. So, I packed up all of my bags, grabbed Joyce in-tow, moved to sunny Orlando, Florida and wrote this book. I hope you enjoyed reading it as much as I enjoyed writing it.

The End

Down through the years with Don King; from his entry into the fight game, when both of our heads grew black hair, on through the internationally renowned relationships with Muhammed Ali and Mike Tyson.

183

ABOUT THE AUTHOR

Vince Sanders is a retired broadcaster with 30+ years as an on-air talent and manager of network operations and local radio station. Migrated in the 1960's from the stage as an actor to work as talk show host and news anchor. Before joining NBC news and subsequently the National Black Network, there were stints with Seaway Broadcasting and Rollins Broadcasting companies in the Chicago area. He is co-founder of the National Association of Black Journalists and past board member of the Central Florida Theatre Alliance.

www.ingramcontent.com/pod-product-compliance
Lightning Source LLC
Chambersburg PA
CBHW030440290526
45786CB00001B/380